About the Author

Clifton I. Seeney, A Navy veteran, tells the story of the life and times of the Seeney Family circa 1920-1940 as told to him by his father, Clifton Samuel Seeney a businessman and a WWII veteran.

About the Book

MEET SARAH GREEN, A Woman of Purpose, is a fictional story and part of an anthology, Big Cliff, based on the life of Clifton Leroy Seeney and the family that was around him in the early part of the nineteenth century.

"Peggy & Clif"

MEET SARAH GREEN

A WOMAN OF PURPOSE

CLIFTON I. SEENEY

Rev. date: 02/15/2016

To order additional copies of this book, contact:
Xlibris
1-888-795-4274
www.Xlibris.com
Orders@Xlibris.com
735790

Introduction

Big Cliff is a fiction, which must be read in the language of the times, based on the life of Clifton Leroy Seeney and the family that was around him in the early part of the nineteenth century.

Many things are based on facts, if at any time the people or a situation seems to be based on actual people it is just a situation and not actual, fact or people.

The Author of the book is the Grandson of Cliff and many of the stories were from his own father. I hope that this book will open the eyes of those who read it. Life in the early part of the nineteenth century or

Life in Baltimore Maryland was never easy for the colored population then as now. We have over come so many things in the past and we will continue to move forward.

I wish to thank most of all Big Cliff for being what he was, also to my Grandmother Gertrude P Seeney, and most of all Sarah Green Tolson.

This book would have not been if it wasn't for my daddy Clifton Samuel Seeney. The help of my editor is without doubt the most important part, for without her help in organizing this work it would have been impossible. Many thanks go out to my sister Peggy Seeney for her help in the background of many of the characters in this story.

Big Cliff II
The Life and times of his Family in the Twenties
By Cliff Seeney

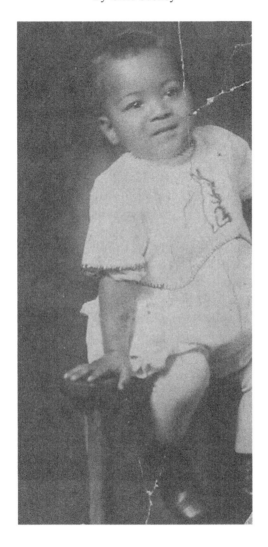

Clifton Samuel Seeney 1923

Like I was saying, Miss Henrietta Seeney was as graceful as a swan. A well educated woman also she was the picture of the new Colored woman, with the manners and charm to go along with it. Her wealth was due to wise investments and the money that her father left her, after years of working as a hood. Carter Solomon Seeney was also receiving Veteran benefit from a wound he received during the Civil War. After some time that benefit went up and he received also the interests off of the arrears from the government.

Miss Henrietta Seeney went to a colored woman's collage called Spellman. She never married and resigned herself to a life of ease. Many people not only admired her for her beauty but for her wise and talented advice. She was, said many, like her Grandfather Samuel W Chase Sr., a well educated man who taught classes at the AME Churches and at the first black schools for free men of color before the Civil War.

When she walked into the room at Miss Sarah's house she was a very welcome guest. Sarah, who handled the care and the upkeep of most of Miss Seeney's houses that were near Franklin Street the 600 block of that Street and other places as well.

All the men there wanted to be near this jewel and they all tried to upstage the others when they had a chance to be near her, which was rare. She rarely came out in public and this was a great opportunity for Sarah to introduce her to her family before they returned back to Virginia.

Sarah was so glade that she got the time to be with her mother and brother. And the fact that her mother got to meet Miss Seeney meant a lot to her. She felt that her life was now turning around and a new way was on its way.

Sarah washed herself all over out in the kitchen across the courtyard behind the house; afterwards she put on her new white dress and her high top city shoes, which were black. The black stockings were a perfect contrast to her new underwear, a style that she was not use to.

She lifted her heavy black hair that she was forming into a bundle and for a woman of forty-two she looked more like a woman of twenty-eight. She now wanted to look younger so she tied it back in a long pony tail, no doubt to show off her wavy hair to any envies eyes.

All the time she was dressing she was thinking of her Mother and Brother who were still in Baltimore. They came to stay for a short while mostly to see the new baby boy that was born to their granddaughter and Cousin. She was wishing that they would stay and hoping that her sister would come up as well. They were very generous to the whole family giving money, to Gurtie for the new baby boy that was born the first of the year.

He looked like a little papoose, just as cute as any Native American baby, just a little darker due to his black heritage.

She was thinking that she felt that his blood was very close because his mother and father were second cousins.

Oh, I will pray that he turns out right but I will keep a close eye on him, during his childhood, she thought to herself.

She knew that it was a common practice for her people to marry in this way. She recalled in her mind that the only way that most Native Americans would be able to get off of the many Reservations, that the white government set up for them, was marrying into the families of the many colored people living near these places was one way.

These Reservations were set up to keep them in confinement, more like a prison than a home. The only way off of the white ran Reservations was to marry someone outside of the tribes. Many whites refused to marry them, but free blacks and Mulattoes were more than willing to add them to their families. Along with this, the ones that wanted to keep their Native American heritage alive often intermarried within their own mixed family.

Once she came to Baltimore she discovered that they too were practicing a form of this in their Quadroon Balls, as they were known. Where young Mulattoes and well to do blacks girls went to a special Ball were young Mulattoes and well to do black young men and many wealthy aristocratic whites came too.

They would pick out the best to be their mistress and in the case of the Mulattoes and the blacks they would pick out wives. This was a good way unlike home to not marry close in the family. Poor Cliff and Gurtie could not do this because their families had neither the money nor the social connection to do so.

Cliff's mother made a arrangement with her family at home to marry him off too one of the families in Virginia the Tolson's, who were not Laws, so I guess she thought that it was alright to do. Her fathers twin sister's son's daughter.

Sarah remembered that her own marriage was an arrangement. She actually wanted to go to one of the balls here to see for herself if there was someone for her Hattie who was turning twenty now and Zep.

The ballrooms were very beautiful and glittering with a thousand lights, the girls wore white dresses, the young men were very light and handsome some were lighter then her Zep, but she felt that they were not as handsome as her son.

She felt that there was nothing evil or wicked about the balls. Indeed, they were conducted with great propriety. The girls were chaperoned by their mothers. When a young man wished to select one as a wife or a mistress he would consult with that girls mother, or get his father to do so, as was often the case. If he was accepted he must make certain promises, among them one of some financial arrangement with her family. He must also be able to provide, too, for the children that might be born of this union. All of the girls would have to prove that they were virgins.

This she thought would be the way she wanted her other girls to go and her sons, but she knew in her heart that this was the high society of Baltimore Maryland, that she did not belong too. As she left the ball she saw her friend serving dinners to the young men and she waved at her, catching herself at the same time. This was not her world and in no way close to her world.

She was thinking about Jack and she felt that she did want to remarry. She would marry Jack and her children would be pleased with it. Then she started to think about his family and how they would receive her, his mother was always nice and polite to the colored people that came to Saint Mary's for prayer and for help. But marriage to an older colored woman was a different matter she thought to her self.

Would she see her beauty or would she see only her age and color?

As she was bringing in the coffee from the kitchen to the round table in the parlor where the family was sitting and eating, she heard her mother bring the subject up about the other children. As all who were there listened attentively, her face was serious and interested.

"Tell me child what do you have planned for these my children?" speaking of Hattie and Zep and little Mary who was now eight years old. "What are they to do if something, the Lord forbid happens to you? Yes, it is true that Gurtie has a good man but what of these my other children." her mother said.

Sarah on the other hand was in deep thought thinking of Jack, he is just a poor white carpenter, she thought to herself, not listening to her mother's speech to the family. She began to fan herself and began drinking some of the wine that Cliff brought in.

Sarah knew in her heart that her own mother kept a deep dark secret in her own pass. Sarah knew that she was next to the youngest of nine children. Her father has long been dead; her own mother was like her twenty years younger than her father. The families that live a few farms from them were kin to the Laws family when Margaret Tolson married into the Taliaferro family.

Now she knew that she, Mary and Lucy were her mother's daughters, but her older brothers were ten years older than they were and her mother was just ten when Dennis was born and thirteen when Robert was born and another sister as well.

"I tell you what I will do," said Cliff, I will make sure all of us are taken care of and if any member of our family needs help, we will all help out in any way we can. Do we all agree? If not I say here and now, that person must leave the family and never be spoken of by any one in this family, do we all agree?" From the Laws family to the Monroe's to the Seeney's to the Chase family they all took a pact between themselves. The Greens and the Tolson's were all included in the pact.

Sarah filled her glass before she answered, "I will not marry." she said to a room full of astonished faces. For she was deep in her own thoughts!

"Where did that come from?" her mother asked her "Child you are too old to marry, there's nothing in you to bring forth on this earth." she said to her".

Cliff said, "I will find suitable husbands for them Miss Green, not to worry."

4

"Such a bold remark." said his half brother to him "Who would you pick for me?" said Robert "Hattie?" "No, that's to close to the blood, I'm the only one that is married too close, let me be the last." he said

"The Chase family has great position and owns much. Will they stay with this pact you made?" said Al and Ed Laws.

"That's very true but, Uncle Al and Uncle Ed you have many daughters don't you and they have many sons and there's no blood between you and them." said Cliff

"There's only blood between the Tolson's the Laws and the Monroe's. No one can marry them. Only outside of them, the Greens and the Chase families are ok to marry. No Seeney can marry a Chase as well and since I'm the only Seeney I will make sure that my sons keep the law as well as my daughter."

Once he said daughter that brought some up raised heads!

The cowpeas were wrapped carefully in a handkerchief and hidden in the bosom of her dress so that Jack would not see them, she hurried across Eutaw Street. As usual he was already at their meeting place; this was a Saturday morning before the rest of the family was up. The weather was very calm for a February day. She told him quickly, sadness was in her speech and in her eyes as every word she said felt like a knife stabbing her in the heart. Jack asked her "Why?" with remorse, in every word he said. Changing this sad moment, he said that his mother was doing better after she took the medicine that Sarah had given him.

He then caught her as she tried to leave, then they both cried rocking in each others arms. They didn't care if the early morning market people stared and whispered and a few giggled at them.

Of course he was upset and let down about what he always knew in his heart, that they would never be husband and wife. "We can still be together my dear." she said through the tears in her eyes. "Yes we can." he said back to her

Once she returned home, another sad sight awaited her; the white Doctor that Cliff knew was leaving her house. "What is wrong!" she asked of him.

"Cliff came and got me this morning to take a look at your mother." he said. "Your mother was in agony since before noon, and now, at last" the Doctor said, "she is doing some what better."

Sarah looked into his soul and saw it was devoid of faith or any trust.

"She most go into the Hospital." He said

Once she was inside she told her mother what the Doctor had said her Mother replied "No"!

There was only one Hospital for colored people and it was runned by them Haitians. She knew that it was not far from them, up and to the east on the four hundred unit block of West Biddle Street.

"No" she also replied to the family that was standing in the small house. "We live with them people on this block and for generations we were treated badly by these French speaking people. Yes, many of them are Mulattoes also but white Mulattoes!" She said "also I know of very few if any old people coming out of Providence Hospital alive."

Cliff said "She will need great care if you want her to recover!"

"You need to speak more respectful to your elders." she said back at him. "You city people know nothing about taking care of the sick!" she told him.

That's when Cliff started to step back from the front of the family. "You take care of the money, I will take care of the people." she said with determination! "What will you do mama?" said Gurtie

"Get me some fresh onions from the grocery store Zep, the white ones the biggest ones you see." she told him.

Once he got the biggest and the best ones, she peeled them in cold water and not an eye did tears drop. "Put them in a bowl of fresh water and see if we all will be just fine." she said

The next day, as she said her Mother's fever broke and those that were getting sick were now well. As word of this got around more and more colored people were lined up at Sarah's store buying all the onions that they could. Many told her that their family was to sick to pay and that it would seem hopeless.

"Peel them and put them in a stocking, white stocking and see them turn black with this evil that comes every winter." she said to them. When the snow is gone the cold rain brings the Black Death which killed so many.

As she walked to the large downtown wholesale market to order more onions, the first person she saw was Jack.

"It is a great thing that you have done Sarah, the whole bottom is talking about you." he said. "Sarah Green is all you can hear, they call you "The Angel" now, who has come from Heaven to cure the poor people of the flu." as cold smoke came from his lips.

They both began to laugh as they kissed one another in the day light in a crowed market, a white man kissing a colored woman.

As many of the old Jewish people went by looking holding their heads down in discuss at what they just witnessed on a street in Baltimore. The white people were taken back by it and called for the police to arrest them!

Running from the police as if they were young, the lovers found a quite place to continue.

For a moment she gave herself to his mouth, to his lean, strong, carpenter's arms, to the beat of his heart. When she could breathe again she told him that she needed to go to the wholesale market on Pratt Street and order all the white onions that she could get before the word gets out all over the city and there would be none to have.

"Ok" Jack said to her, "I will see you tonight?" he said as he took another kiss from the lips of his love.

Once she got down town to Pratt Street wholesale Market, she found out that there was a run on the sale of white onions. She had a feeling that that was going to happen so before she left the house she asked Cliff to go and see his friend Mr. Albert and get him to get the Cuban ship Captains to bring on the next shipments to Curtis Bay, all the fresh fruits and vegetables that their ships could hold and buy up all that they had.

Cliff asked her where he going to get that much money. Sarah told him to get it from the family and she gave him all the money that she had which was about a thousand dollars.

He collected the same from all the heads of the family and some extra from his half- brothers who were not overjoyed giving up their hard earned money, but it would be better to give it to him than to have a talk with Mr. Jimi.

They at once got in his 1910 model T Ford with Mr. Jimi and some others. They went south on the new Baltimore to Annapolis Road to Curtis Bay where the Cubans had their secret pier set up. He gave the order to Manuel Andres the chief of the Cubans ship captains and he got half of the agreed payment. "Those Cubans drive a hard deal." he said to Mr. Jimi, but with Jimi standing next to him and Mr. Albert they gave in.

It would be early in March before they would return with maybe three ships loaded with food,what would she do till then?

Sarah was the most resourceful woman that Cliff had ever seen, she had the basements of all her buildings on Franklin Street full of cans and jars of fresh fruits and she had bags after bags of potatoes and onions. With so many small grocery stores selling out of fresh food stuff due to the outbreak of flu she was able to corner the market and Mr. Baily started to buy out as many small grocery stores that he could in the Mulberry- Franklin Street area all the way over to Baltimore Street.

Chapter 2

Jack watched as she went down the path cutting though the tall weeds that were choking the area. Then she paused a moment before the door of one of the small shacks that was on this alley street.

He was to far away to hear her knock, but he saw the door open to admit her. She walked through the black rectangle and into what seemed to be darkness.

Once again he was spying on her and he was feeling bad about it. The weather was trying to break and it was the first of the month and it was rent week, she collected the rents for Cliff's Aunt and her own as well. He should have known better he thought to himself, I was just under pressure from the family.

That night she had a dream, she was dreaming that she was dead. She dreamed that her body was floating on a dark river and all about her were other bodies that were floating also. Their eyes were closed and their faces were dead, but she could recognize some of them. She saw her grandmother the proud Powhatan, she saw the old woman that died a few months ago in her rooming house, and she saw Margaret Laws Tolson as well.

She recognized others, too. And there were strangers – many, many strangers. She heard Margaret say, "Why did you let it happen."

She could not catch her breath, she almost died. Wake up mama, wake up mama, was all she could hear, for to her was forever, then she felt wet and knew that someone was trying to reach her.

"Oh Child," her mother said, "don't go away now, there's to much work here for you to do."

Mary had left her and ran and got her Grandmother to wake her. "Are you ill child?" she said very tenderly "you must not think of what you have dreamed it is a vision that your people get, your father used to get them also. God rest his soul. We came up to help you in the vision. My people don't have what your people have as far as vision into the future is concerned."

I was dying, "Sarah told her mother. Perhaps I was dead for a while." As they got her to come down the small stairs, that led her to the front room. She could smell incense that her brother had brought with them, which their father gave them to give to her.

"It will not work for them your brother's child, they are for you, and you are of your father's blood, back to his mother." "No, Mama you are wrong they are not of your blood they are of their own mothers' blood, you need to tell them and let the blood that is holding you down free them." Sarah said.

"Child I know now that you are special and that there is a power in you. Your father said that you would be in danger and that you would need the help of your spirit guide one day, so we hope this will help you to overcome the danger". "Yes, Mama I still remembered how they called you a black nigger because your people were slaves and black!" Mama I want you to be free of that now.

Later that night, she awoke and stretched out her arms. Towards the other side of the bed and felt with longing in the cool sheets of emptiness, and remembered again that he was not there but she was in her own bed.

Within a week she was up and about just like nothing had happen.

That next month, Cliff and the men went driving in his auto down to Curtis bay to pay the Cubans for the ships that were loaded down with food stuff. Robert, his half brother said that this was the craziest thing he ever heard of, fresh fruit in March, man you got to be mad, looking in the back seat at Jimi the whole time that he was talking.

"Man I hope you really know what you are doing." said old man Al Laws who out lived his father (who was dead by the time he turned forty-eight) looking back at his brother Ed as he was talking.

"Man, we all gave a thousand dollar to this man we will be ruined if this don't work!" they said.

"The sickness has long stopped, boys!" Mr. Sam Chase IV said. He was setting next to Cliff in the middle between him and Robert. Just then all six of them laughed at one another. "Man, we just gave Cliff over six thousand dollars."

Why was this happening to her so late in her life, love and knowledge? The whole time she was married to old Zep Tolson, all she did was take care of children and cleaned up after a handless man. Now that she was in love she couldn't marry the man that she was in love with.

Then she recalled how old Zep use to come around on the weekends and get his loving off on her. Just like she was a roadside gal, not remembering that he used to be married to her, tell he found a younger gal to do it with. That was the principal question on her mind.

He was breathing hard on her, "are you, ok?" she asked "yes, I am" he said back to her.

Now she could be certain that he was awake and with her. "I don't understand?" he said to her. "It's better not to think on bad things, dear." she said. "There was no reason for it," she said. "It happens to women." he said "I don't know much about it, Sarah.

And this isn't the time to talk about it." "Then when is it time to talk about it?" She set up in the bed; her feet were pulled under the old quilt that his mother made for him before he went off to the war. I feel that we are being destroyed because of what I permitted him to do." she said. "Yes, I let him send my daughter up here and I could have stopped her from marrying that boy, but I gave in to his hard ways.

The man had no heart everything to him was money." "Hush, baby let's get some rest and not think on this tonight." "Ok" as she turned her broad back to him not kissing him as she normally does.

"What are you going to do with all this fruit amigo?" the Cuban said to Cliff. "It is green now but in a few days it will be brown and no good. I tell you what I will do for you my homme, I will sell it to you for half price and I will bring another load up next month. Si my amigo."

"Ok, what are we going to do now?" Robert looked with surprise in his face and saw trucks, ice trucks that the I-Talins had waiting for them on the out side of the pier? As Mr. Albert's gang of longshoreman unloaded the Ships on too the ice trucks, all kinds of ideas were going off in the six of their minds.

"I got to say Cliff, yea you can get the fruit and the veggies off but where are you going to put them?" "Well, there's an ice house on Mulberry Street and Pulaski Street and the mob controlled it and the fruit can be put in there till I'm told by Sarah what to do with it."

"Oh, God we are ruined!"

"It looked like Cliff had this all planned out till we got back in town." said Robert Monroe".

"Robert you get your A-rads up here every morning and sell them these seconds. I guess Sarah knows what she doing".

The weather for that April started out very warm and then by the middle of the month the rains came, not with any ice but just cold windy weather every day. The days were now split one day sunny the next would be cold and windy the next would be cold and wet.

After the first week of that kind of weather many of the people that didn't catch the flu the first time were coming down with it and the need for white onions was once more in demand. Sarah had all the stores that Mr. Baily had bought stocked with fresh white onions, and they were beginning to sell out but the onions only stopped the fever, the illness was still spreading as the weather got worse for the last three weeks in April, which was the worst that the whole east coast had seen in many years.

The people down in Little Italy had trucks coming up to Mulberry Street that cleaned out all the white onions out of the ice house. Over in the rich neighborhoods of Edmondson Ave the white people who were close to the Ice House bought up most of them. In no time the ice house was empty of fresh fruits and veggies.

What Sarah did was to fill the stores with all the cans and jars of fresh fruit that she had that the woman folk made out of the last shipment of fresh fruit. Uncle Roberts's boys were busy selling the seconds that were left in the ice house. Never in the history of the city could you buy an orange in April or a watermelon that wasn't at a rich mans restaurant. By the end of the month the weather was the same and it looked like it was going to snow on Easter morning but the Cubans ships were in and the trucks were loading up.

There was trouble down at Curtis Bay; the police were closing down the pier, without letting anymore trucks on to the Pier. Not before Cliff and his I-Tlains friends loaded up all their trucks, but this time the mob took the biggest share of the food. Not only did they take the biggest share but they sent mob boys to Cuba to run the shipping business there.

Chapter 3

It was the day after Easter and the moon was full. It blazed down through the gnarled branches of the live oak trees. It silvered the branches, and it brightened the pools of water left by the cold rains of the late winter. If you were out and about on this night your skin would have shine, beyond the moon the stars were a blaze, it seemed almost with anger.

Many people were coming from or going to the sunrise services that many of the Churches were having. Many were full with joy on this night knowing that they were spared and saved from the death and pain of the last wave of the killer flu season. Many owed their life to the helping hands of Sarah Green's family and many gave thanks to our family but like all things you had those that could care less.

Note: please read Dorothy Daugherty, Sharp Street Church historian, on her first experience of segregation.

In the morning Sarah awakened with a dull headache and a feeling as if she had been drugged.

The dreams were coming more than ever, she could barely remember them but the after effect still was there. The perfume of the incense helped to quiet the dreams but also took the memory of them away.

She was long in gathering her consciousness together, and then she first thought of Jack and not of the visions.

Each morning her first thoughts were of him, she had an impulse to call out to him, aloud, as if he was there in the room with her. Then she started too smile at herself, lying there in her bed, with her head still aching. She began to recall in her mind that many saints aided those who could not help themselves, no I'm not a saint and far from being one she thought. But why did the sprits want me to do these things? There in her room were many colored candles, black, brown, green and white, purple and pink. What do they mean and who brought them in here, she questioned herself?

She felt strange when she crossed the wide commons that people were beginning to call the division between colored and white, old from new. In the white neighborhoods most of the buildings were very ugly to her, for nearly all of them were red brick, instead of the tinted and painted in delicate pastel shades of pink and blue and lavender, as was on Orchard Street just like you were in New Orleans. She thought that was the only good thing that the Haitians brought to the area.

In the White areas there were very few that had front and back gardens, the ones that did were all in the back and they seemed huge, but crude and sprawling, unlike the lovely courtyards in the colored part of town.

The prize flower was the peony in the colored part of town, and in the white it was the rose. Any one could pick a peony that lasted just one day, but the thorns of the rose kept many from picking them. Very few of the streets had cobblestones or proper banquettes. And in many places the passing autos had to ride through mud and standing water, particularly if it had rained lately, and the pedestrians often went ankle- deep in the slime. As always she felt that the white Americans knew nothing about how to live. Some of the many white people who had poured into the city after the war in the past few years have become rich.

With the sale of the old houses in the older part of the city and the high rents that the white landlords were charging people were getting richer by the day on the backs of the many white and the new colored people that were coming up from the south looking for their streets paved with gold.

The Jewish people were the only ones that didn't move out of the old areas, mainly because of their religion.

Many of the Jewish people still lived next to colored from the unit block up to the 1000 block of Druid Hill Ave. but as the old colored people said; all they cared for was the making of money. Many of the newly arrived whites would be overheard by their colored servants as saying that they did not intend to stay, and they thought that the latest illness was brought up here by the poor coloreds from the south. They said that when they were rich enough they would return back to the south and rebuild the south as it was before the rebellion.

15

Sarah picked her way through the narrow and muddy Streets that made up the North Ave area; she had a growing disdain as she continued to walk. She thought that this whole area was white and every one that she passed was white, she would hear every now and then, "Look at the nigger!" As if she was an amusement to them.

She was wondering why some of them light skinned colored people were trying to move up here and why Mr. Perry Chase Jr. would want to have an establishment put in this part of town. Many colored people were now working up here and using the back alleys to move up and down coming and going to work. They were using the side streets as if they were rodents hiding from the view of the white people. She felt that it was shameful how some of these black people were acting, some were even drunk and it was before noon.

"Hey lady, I'll give you a dollar for your time!" as if all colored woman were road side gals. Sarah now was walking faster, and with more than usual hauteur, for she knew how these white people felt about a light skinned colored woman. Many of them could not distinguish one of us from the other, a quadroon from a Negro, a poor southern dark skinned Negro from a rich northern colored person. With the people that grew up south of North Ave. it was different, and she was thankful that there was a few up here. Once she got to Mr. Bernstein's place she was so relieved that he was Jewish and he treated her better than that poor white trash that she passed on her way to his Law offices.

Mr. Bernstein could have not been more polite. He ushered her into his office and at once offered her a chair. He was a stout and nervous little man, when he spoke he paced the floor. He asked her what he could do for her. She told him that her son-in-law cousin sent her to see him. Then she told him who he was. It was Mr. Perry Chase Jr. of the Samuel W Chase Jr. Funeral homes that is when he set down and started to relax some what.

"Yes," he said to her "I do a lot of legal work for them." "Mr. Bernstein, I need you to put these properties in legal deeds and to do legal work for my family."

It was very usual for white Lawyers to do such work for colored people in the 1920's, there were colored Lawyers doing all the legal work for them. Most of the Lawyers that were doing legal work lived on Division Street or up in the 1000 block of Druid Hill Ave.

He told her that there was a good boy up on Druid Hill that he could send her too, by the name of Callaway. She replied, "why would I use a boy, to do a man's job!" "Ok, Miss I understand, yes I do."

She said, "I need a Lawyer who knows the Judges and the political leader's downtown."

She watched this little ball headed man as he was fumbling in a metal box that was on his desk. He then laid some bills out then he told her that if she could come up with a thousand dollars he would do all and any legal work for her family. As, soon as he said that, she tossed, the money down on his desk! With an unbelieving look on his face he said "I heard of you, you're Sarah Green aren't you? She smiled, this famous Lawyer had heard of her. "Yes, I'm she." "Miss Green I will do it for half of what I said. You, Miss Green are an angel sent by the Angel Michael, which spared my family during the flu season." he said.

Then he explained to her what happened.

"My family has many members that are still down on the unit blocks of McCullah Street and after their servant told them of you they laughed, till one after the other came down with the flu. Many were near death till Miss Ruth; their colored servant brought from your store on Druid Hill them large white onions. She peeled them and put them in every sick room in every house that we owned, even my wife and children got sick and the Doctors said that there was nothing they could do but let the fiver run its course."

That's when he got on his knees and started praying in Hebrew in front of her. "Oh, Miss Green I owe you so much please I beg you take back all your money I will be your servant till we are called home to God!" he said. "If you ever need anything my house is yours and all that I have is yours."

"Mr. Bernstein that's a whole lot that you said, but I tell you what I'll do, I will pay you what you ask for but I will hold you to what you said, and if you break your word let's just say what came this season will come again and again my good man."

She recalled what her father told her about what his mother told him. How the Powhatans cared for the whites when they came to their lands and how just like him said that they would do almost the same thing. Later they turned on the Native Americans and took their lands and all that they owned and put them in small camps that had smallpox, and many other illnesses.

"No, I will keep my word." he said to her "We will see." she said to him.

Chapter 4

Cliff was mad as he could be with the people down in little Italy, for what they had done and what they were doing at Curtis Bay.

He felt that they betrayed him some way and that he had an oath by the King of the mob that he was his God son.

He looked at Jimi and said "we are going to take a trip and get this settled one way or another".

With his temper up he packed his bags, kissed the baby and told Gurtie that he and Mr. Jimi were going on a little trip and for her not to worry. "Honey, I want you to take care of the books till I get back, see if you can straighten them out for me. Also things don't seem to be balancing out." he said to her.

Once again he used Uncle Zep as a white man, they dressed him up much better this time.

They made so much money off the fruits and veggies that they all started to wear new suites just like them white businessman. They looked so good that most of the people in the block came out to see them on this fine Easter morning.

"My, oh, my" said Miss Woodford, as they stood next to the new car that they got.

"I have never seen colored men look so good. Is that you Zeppy?" asked Mrs. Massey the Jewish lady that lived near the end of the block. "You are going up north and start passing (for white) aren't you she asked."

"Boy, you better not open your mouth they will know that you're a colored man for sure." she said.

Then her fat husband said, "Yea, they hang naggers, for that up there!" as he closed his door with a slam.

Once they got to Penn Station Zep went to the ticket booth and got three tickets in the sleeping car for one white man and two colored musicians.

Cliff knew that someone might recognize him, so Cliff stayed in the sleeping coach while Jimi and Zep set in the white only car.

Now this was truly amazing in the segregated era, for not only them but to all the white folks. That this, black man was setting by such a well dress white man in a white only coach!!!

But, as the story goes the conductor tried to move Jimi out of his seat till he looked into them cold black eyes of Jimi. And when the rest of them white people did the same they all just let it be!

Now I really believe that this man had a power over people, because he was too short to even scare a fly, let alone all the people that came in contact with him in his early years. And he could not weigh no more than one- ten when I was a boy. Well any way they got to Chicago with out any trouble.

And since they did this once before they knew just were to go. Now I tell you, I would not have done what they were doing once but two times would have been two too many. This time ole Al was there, now this was just by luck and I tell you these boys had a pocket full of luck.

"Yea, can we a help you boys" said the body guard (out side the office building were the Chicago mob had their headquarters),

"Yea, Boss, my Boss wants to speak to his Godfather?

"He's a got a Godfather, you coons, better get away from here before you be a swinging from an old oak tree!" said the mob goon.

Zep told this tale as follows: just then Jimi jumps in front of that big I-Tilian and puts his hand in his coat and said, "My boss wants to talk to his Godfather."

Well that big I-Tilian looks up to a window and two more big I-Tilians came down to the front of the building. "Hey, niggers, what you a want here? Didn't he tell you to get lost?"

Just then little Jimi pulls open his coat and shows the I-Tilian a Tommy gun that he had under his coat, now this was in broad daylight in the windy city. So those I-Tilians just got madder than hell. One said, "Look the monkey has a gun, oh, we are so afraid!"

"What's going on here?" you could hear from the inside of the building. "You bozo's got nothing better to do?" the voice said.

"No Boss, we were just having fun with these here colored boys". "What colored boys you a talking about let me see".

"Hey Cliff, how you doing! What you doing here, you bozos get to your post. I'll deal with you dummies later." Said Mr. Nitti

"I asked them, could I talk to my Godfather and your boys wouldn't let us, so my man here had to show them that we meant business." said Cliff.

"Ok, I take you up to see the Boss myself." "Thanks Frank, for the help." said Cliff

"Ok, Cliff I told you if I had men that could think on their feet like you I wouldn't have to do everything myself!"

"What's wrong Cliff?" "Well Frank, I had a problem with your boys down in Baltimore, so much that I had to come up here and see if we could come to a better arrangement." "Hey, Cliff, is ah you talking about that new company business that we got down there in Cuba?"

"Oh, yea, that's it. How did you know about that?" said Frank Netty to Cliff. "Well you see we had a secret pier in Curtis bay (to make a long story short)." Cliff told him his story. "I was a figuring that, that Ole Don in Baltimore couldn't have done that on his own." said Frank. "Here Cliff I take care of this for you we don't need to trouble the Boss with this ok. I owe you one ok Cliff." said Mr. Frank. "Ok, Frank I trust you."

"Let's go boys!" "Hey, wait a little bit take this card down town to any restaurant and show it." he said "Have a good meal on me, ok."

With that and a good meal the boys were off back to Baltimore but not before more adventure awaited them.

Sarah felt fortunate that her deed during the past sickness was spreading her name through out town, it was now a different world from what she was use to in Virginia. Down there she was just someone to be used.

After she got back down to her house she and her friend Gail got together and sanctified Gail's new home, using the candles that she had. She lit a pink one for love and peace and a white one for life and health and the green one for money.

"Girl, where did you learn this?" her friend Gail asked. "You know my peoples were from New Orleans." Gail said "No I didn't know that!" "Yea girl and they used them candles just like you did. Now I know by hairdressing undertaking will be a success."

Once Sarah returned home her mother was setting in the rocker in which she had been resting herself and flung her arms over her head with a passionate gesture, "Well child, it's time for us to head back home. You take care now and keep an eye on that baby I feel that he will grow wicked if you don't it's just to close, child to close."

Sarah had a talk with Gail the next day and Gail said "I know that you are clever with hair and I know that together we can open up a shop down here and get them up town niggers to come down here and get them knots busted and them curls straightened.

We can put waves all over them ladies hair and make them look like movie picture stars. I saw you with your daughters you used great skill in putting their hair up. And when I'm gone up town to them white folk's houses you can run the shop with your gal's." "Oh, Gail, don't say that, I wouldn't know what to do without you."

"You go on now!" said Gail to her. "You think know body knows that you got a man, but I do and I know that he is white. I seen you sneaking out every night, you think them Gal's of yours don't know. I'm telling you as a friend that they know and there's nothing wrong with that. Me, and you aren't no Saints, I will set on some of my own customer's husband's laps every now and then, when they want some dark meat. That is in their house and they don't have to run down town and get no road side Gal. Now I told you, are we still friends gal?"

"Yes, we are." as both of them laughed at one another. So Sarah had two trades now running the stores and doing hair, her style of dress changed as well.

'Honey, you just to pretty to be down here' she would hear every time she went into Cliff's place to get a glass of beer. The women in the bar were just a bunch of dusty road side gal's trying to pick up a trick and the other women; well they looked like they were working.

Just about anything and everything was coming to Sarah's lunch room now that was because of the kind of people that were going to Cliff's place now.

Gurtie was busy taking care of the books for her husband and the books for the road houses that were up on US Route #1.

That little baby boy was getting bigger now and cute as he could be. "I want him to stay in my house." Sarah told Gurtie, "he's to big now and there is just too much going on in that bar for him to see with them young eyes."

"Ok Mama, you are right, I'll pick him up on the weekdays when it quit down in there and I bring him over on Friday to you." "Ok Child, that sounds good."

Chapter 5

It was a long time before Sarah would see Mr. Bernstein. Then on a Sunday in May of 1920 as she was taking an afternoon walk, she heard the sound of music coming from Lafayette Square. Mr. Bernstein was standing there listening to the music that the Jazz band was playing; it was Jelly Roll Morton and his band in Baltimore.

"Well, well of all the places to find you, a great Lawyer like you down here listening to Jazz, I thought you were a stiff collard Jew!"

"Well, if it ain't the Widow Tolson."

"Sarah Green to you thanks you very much." Sarah did not wonder at his uncertainty, for she knew she looked like a very different woman from the one he had seen some month's ago. She remained some feet away, watching him but feeling odd and shy as she glanced at this short and balding man. She wore a simple long dress this Sunday in May. The color was blue and it was layered with a blue calico apron that wrapped around her now full figure. Not the overly full figure of the large burly black woman that you might see doing the laundry for the rich, but the nice pear shape of a maturing woman. There was grace in her walk and her smile would launch a thousand ships.

"It's good to see you Mr. Bernstein," she said very politely. Standing together, they both returned their attention to the dancers and the music.

The square was jammed with celebrants, and in the center stood Jelly Roll Morton, not dancing or playing his piano but singing, now as if he was singing to her. Sarah knew that she was often looked at by other man as this famous band leader was looking at her; she began to stand like a statue while the others whirled about her. The other musicians saw their leader move toward the woman in the blue dress, among them was a soon to be famous trumpet player from New Orleans.

Mr. Bernstein was beginning to feel foolish as all the attention in the square was now on them. Sarah shrugged. "It gives them pleasure. It's an amusement. She asked him did he come to these concerts often, "No, I just started to come after I saw you" "Oh", as he caught himself. "I was given an invitation by Mr. Wilson! Mr. Elroy Wilson."

"I don't think I know him." "Oh he works with your Son- in- Laws Uncle, Mr. Chase."

"I was often invited to attend, but I always had something else to do." she said. She saw Gail now, and another woman that was with her who acted cool towards her as they approached them.

"Hey gal, I see you got out of the house and away from that man of yours, who's your friend Sarah?" "Oh, this is my Lawyer, Mr. Bernstein."

He added, "Herman Bernstein Esq."

"Please to meet you Sir", Gail said "Might need me one of them Lawyers myself one day if I get as rich as Ole Sarah here!" laughing at them.

The other woman was beside herself with envy looking at Sarah and her long Black hair, "is that a wig, gal?" she asked. "No that's my own hair." Sarah said.

"Oh, you must be an Indian then?" said the other woman to Sarah. "No" said Sarah to her "my father's mother was one though" Sarah laughingly said.

Perhaps this woman with Gail knew some of Gail's clients who had been coming to Gail's new shop on Green Street.

Mrs. Fordham was a new and wealthy client and Gail wanted them to know just maybe the Lawyer might know who she was? Yes, as she just dropped the ladies name hoping for a good reply from the Lawyer.

"I do know that Lady" said Mr. Bernstein to Gail, "she is very wealthy and is very loose." which was unusual for a white man to say in front of colored people.

"She is," said Gail "um". "I know her well." he said, "I do work for her estates every now an then."

"Are you from this side of town?" Gail asked of him. "Oh, no I grew up in East Baltimore on Baltimore Street near Central Ave." he said. "Oh, do tell" said Sarah, for Gail was taking up way to much of his time for her liking. "I talk to you later gal." as she ushered Mr. Bernstein to another part of the court.

They walked together toward downtown near the Mayfair Theater.

"Oh!" He said looking up at the Marquee, "Do you or would you like to join my family and see this Opera? It is by a colored playwright and a famous songwriter by the name of Mr. Scott Joplin." he said to her". She thought and said "By all means, yes, I would love to join your family at the white only Theater on Howard Street." "I will come by your house and pick you up in my family car next Sunday."

She was thinking to herself that with Jack, she never went any where but his bed and even then it was in secrecy, hiding from everyone and doing things only at night, why? Could it be that Jack was shamed to be seen with a colored woman in the day or was it something she didn't know?

The theater would be a great solace for her and a great opportunity to be out in the public, even if it meant that she would be looked on as just a servant of a rich Lawyers family.

The mere fact that he was picking her up at her own home was something wonderful and new to her for so many years she was used just as a Fille de joie by every man that she has known; she knew that she wasn't, but her looks and figure made men act that way towards her. If she was a white woman she would be a star among them, but as a colored woman plus poor and a half–breed, she was used and abused.

Sarah had no idea that many colored people were advancing to high places in the theater nowadays, as well as in all the arts? There were great actresses and actors in Europe that were of colored backgrounds. She knew that she had very little education and her use of the English langue was limited as while. There were many things that separated her from other colored women, she would look at Cliff's Aunt and see that as while.

Henrietta Seeney had all the education that was open to a well to do colored woman and the family name. She had the style of the high Society, plus the manners of that class. There was an air about her that kept people from imposing on her, for most people knew that they were not like her and could never be like her.

Sarah also knew that, being just two years younger then her she felt great respect for Miss Seeney, as did everyone else, including her own brother Isiah.

Now she thought to herself it's time to change her ways and enjoy her new found fame, no more hiding in corners and meeting in secret, if Jack wanted her he had to come out in the open and she would not be bound to her children any more.

I want to be free of this old way of living and become a modern woman, she thought to herself.

She thought to herself, 'would there be any one else in her life besides Jack?' She thought that Mr. Bernstein was now no more than someone who worked for her and that she was paying him, not to confuse her mind with romantic notions. Although he was the first man in a long time that asked her to a show and not to her bed, to her that had merit. He is a married man and she was finding out that he was a fine man. Jack, on the other hand, was a soldier who served with Black Jack Pershing during the Spanish American war and with him in Mexico with the 10th Buffalo Soldiers, as a Sergeant in the all black unit. Where as Mr. Bernstein was always a money groping Jew.

I'm too young to always live by myself taking care of children. My youngest is now eight years old and she knew that no one believed that Mary was Zep Tolson's child, but she knew better, that man catted around more than a Tom cat in his day. It might be because of that black straight hair of his, (that he inherited from his Grandmother Margaret Mann); she thought he was such a Tom cat. After all he was married twice before she married him and after he divorced her he got married again. He had about thirteen kids that she knew of, now his twin brother was lighter and only had one wife and a son she thought to herself!

Sarah was amusing herself as she thought of these things, and she laughed at herself. I know exactly what I'm going to do!

The next day she was talking to Gail, "Sarah, you need a man, a good man. I know you love Jack, but what good is he to you here and he is there. You need a man that's going to support you, give you things take you places, and do something more than just bed you." she said. "Now that Lawyer he's got money and I see that he likes you a lot. Now if that was me gal I hitch my cart to him fast before some other filly gets her hands on his money, gal"!

Mr. Frank Moore was a small dark wiry man, who kept pacing Sarah's floor talking nervously but seemingly unable to reveal to her the purpose of his visit.

Sarah rocked patiently, thinking why does time goes so slow, each day seemed like forever and each hour seemed like a day. Knowing that in time she would discover whatever it was that had brought him to her house. Patiently, she prompted him. "You are a very old friend of Miss Seeney, Sir?"

"Yes, a very old friend" said Mr. Frank.

She said, "No, she vows you helped her."

"Yes, I did. Well Miss Sarah, I need your help also and I will pay you handsomely if you manage my buildings down in SoBo and in Pig Town." he said. "You see Miss Sarah; my family has been in Baltimore more than two hundred years. We were slaves that were freed and then my families master gave them land in them places. But I'm too old to keep them buildings up that my people built on that land. And I have no living relations left after the flu of 09 and this year. Only the extremity of my circumstances has driven me to come here."

"You do flatter me." she said

"Pardon, I intended no insult."

"It is nothing, Sir, You are upset." Mr. Frank closed his eyes.

"I am distraught. Do you read the newspapers Sarah?"

"Almost never," she said. "I do not read very well, and all I need to know is from gossip about in the streets these days."

The little man sank into a chair and covered his eyes with his hands. When he took away his eyes were wet. "It is my son his name is William and he is to be tried for murder tomorrow," he blurted out. "Have you not heard that in the streets? He is my only flesh n blood in this God forsaken city. It was in self-defense. The other man was a hoodlum, running them policy slips out of the First Baptist Church for them Mason's. He is all that I have in this world! I had this colored attorney, but they have little hope for him. I have done everything I could for him but he ran around with them policy boys. Miss Sarah if you can help me I will reward you well." He sprang to his feet and began walking up and down again. "You live here in this small crowded house. I will give you one of my own houses on McCullah Street, it's a three story house with a servants place in the basement that leaves out to the street and it's a corner lot with a large back yard. I have little money left but I will give you that house if you will help save my son."

"Calm yourself and tell me what happened, Mr. Moore. I must know the details so that I will know what to do for your son."

The tale Mr. Moore told was rather ordinary. The killing had occurred in a bar in SoBo.

There had been a quarrel over some winning numbers that his son was responsible for and the other man refused to pay him and pulled a razor on him. His son in defending himself got the better of the other man and cut that man across the neck. The police asked no questions and the young man was taken to jail and was now waiting for his day in court. The old man was beside himself. She asked him the name of the man that was killed he said he think it was Harris or Smith he wasn't quite sure but she heard that the man killed was from the south and he was a rouge who tried using his size to bully people, not well liked and he was known to not pay off on his policies.

Where he was killed was like him a cesspool of low life. In the corner of Sharp Street owned by a Jew that sold cheap wine and moon shine and water downed beer to drunken black men and cheap street gal's.

"The police no doubt were paid off by this Jew. I think that I will have your son home in no time." She said.

The little man sprang to his feet. "Can you be sure? I swear the house I promised will be yours!"

"Oh, it will be mine you know who my Son-in-Law is don't you." she said

"Oh, yes I do. Big Cliff!" he said.

"Go now and go in peace." she replied to him.

The next day she had Robert Monroe go up on North Ave. to Mr. Bernstein's law office with a request for him to come at once to her house to talk over some important legal matters.

Mr. Bernstein was more than happy to see her again and wasted no time in getting into his auto and drove down to see her.

"I came as fast as I could1!" he told her, holding her hand in his. "We are still on for the play Sunday?" he asked her with a worried look on his face, his anxiety was showing all over his face.

She never felt this way about him but she could tell that he was highly taken by her.

"I have a favor to ask you and it must be done this month." she said to him.

"Pray, tell me what do you want me to do?" he said.

"I need you to get Mr. William Moore off of a murder charge; can you do that for me?

"I will try." he said

She told him all about it and told him if he did this she would be beholding to him. That night she prayed that the truth would be known!

Sunday finely came and Sarah was so thrilled so much in fact she broke a date with Jack and refused to tell her children till the last minute when Mr. Bernstein's family was parked in front of her house. All the neighbors on Orchard Street were standing on the side walk (the cobble stoned road that the city called a Street). Many would peak out of closed blinds and behind curtains. Over at Cliff's Bar the drunks and the regulars came out to view also, even Big Cliff with his glasses falling down his hooked nose.

Later that month the trial went fast and to the surprise of all that were there when they saw a well known and highly respected Lawyer such as Herman Bernstein. They just looked dumbfounded because of the degree of knowledge the Lawyer for the defense had. The state had no witnesses and they could not call on the arresting policeman because of their reputation as Negro hatters and members of the KKK in Maryland. The case as Sarah said went only a few hours if that long and was thrown out of the court.

Happy with such a fast trial, Mr. Bernstein's office was loaded with colored people trying to get him to do legal work for them. His clients use to be all Jewish and now he had a much larger base to work with so much so that he thought of using colored Lawyers in his new Law firm.

Big Cliff on the left 1920

Chapter 6

"Do Gods works, and not the devils or, perhaps the devil can be made to work for the Lord?" Sarah told Gail. "Any way; I must do the work I have been called to do."

Near them was an old black woman was ease dropping on what they were talking about and jumped from her chair yelling, "Blasphemy, blasphemy, you gal's need the Lord in your lives I'm going to lay hands on you and save your souls!" said the old woman.

"What in the world is that ole fool talking about?" said Sarah to Gail.

"Girl, now days, all these ole people seem to do now is going around trying to save as many people as they can before they die, they think that will get them into Heaven!"

"Yea, I hear you Gail, you know they have done so much in their own lives when they were young now they think they can work their way into Heaven by laying hands on people and leading them to Jesus." "Gal I know a cute Preacher down the way that I kind know personal like." said Gail.

"My word don't let that ole bag hear that, we will never get her out of our hair!" as they both laughed and threw up their skirts at that poor ole woman.

"You gal's, I will pray for you." said that poor ole soul to them and she laughed also saying, gal go change them dirty underwear." laughing at them.

"I know she's not talking to me!" said Gail.

"Well if the shoe fits you got to wear it?" said Sarah laughing at Gail!

Cliff was now working very hard to keep the bar free of wino's and drunks, he got a new guy to act as a bouncer in the bar on the weekends when them types seem to come around just like flies on dung. That ole boy came from a place in the country called Elkridge; his name was Charles Smith, a big ole brown skin boy with tight hair, so tight that Al Laws couldn't cut. But, he was good in putting out them drunks and keeping them street gal's out of the bar on the weekends. During the week Gurtie would take care of the lunchroom and the Afro-American people who were their best customers. Like all newspaper people they just talked on and on about every thing which Gurtie would go back and use the news that she picked up from the newspaper people in her own conversation when the woman folk got together. A new lady was introduced to the group her name was Hazel Scott a good friend of Gurtie. She met Miss Scott at the road house on Route One with Cliff, they became fast friends. Miss Scott took a liking to that ole boy Charles and they were always seen eating together at the Lunchroom.

Sometimes in the day ole Robert would come by with his chickens and eggs and Hazel and Gurtie would be seen cleaning those white Leg Horn chickens in the courtyard of Big Cliff's Place. Now that her mother, Sarah, lived up on McCullah Street in them rich folk's neighborhood, she wasn't around her and her sisters like she use to be. The only time that she got to spend any time with them was when she had free time to run down to the grocery store and her mothers Lunchroom down from the bar and when she would pick up baby Cliff on Mondays.

Sarah now had many trades; she was a caregiver and a businesswoman plus a hairdresser. The big house that she was given had six bedrooms, a large living room which was equal in size to the huge dinning room, plus the kitchen, which was once the kitchen to a wealthy family that fell on hard times before the civil war. They left the home to their slaves the Moor's before running to the South with whatever money that they could get to help in the Rebellion.

The downstairs was the quarters for twenty or so Slaves, which not only worked in this house, but also was used in their holdings above North Ave in the Reisterstown road area.

Many of the slaves that they had, all but their favorite house slaves the Moor's, were sold down south to support the cause.

Now Sarah was using it for her Beauty shop. With Gail and another they set up shop there where white as while as colored were customers, at separate times of course. This in many ways kept her romance with Jack still in the hide and sake mode for the time being.

Her social meeting with the Bernstein's family was growing so much so that she was a welcome guest at dinner with that family. She often took her children uptown past North Ave. to the Reisterstown road area were the Bernstein's family had a large home near the new Druid Hill Park on Brookfield Ave. In the new auto that she bought that Uncle Zep drove for her.

Now Uncle Zep was a real smooth guy, he learned early that it was better playing the part of a white person than colored, in the 1920's. He moved through both races as easy as a piece of butter on hot cakes. He knew when to speak and when not to, he made friends with both black and white people and he often went as a Native American whenever he could to find ways around the ways of America in the 1920's. He would go to meetings to see what was going to happen in what area of town that was close to colored people. Often he would meet others like himself and they would just laugh it off.

To them white people were just crazy in the way they acted towards the colored people of this world often his buddies would get involved with the most prejudice people just to laugh at them and their colored grandchildren.

Once one of his friends made the leader of the SoBo pig town KKK so hoping mad that if it wasn't for the fact that there were so many colored people living in Baltimore now he would have hung that ole boy.

While life in the big city was changing a lot of people, and crime was one thing that many of these country people were not use to. They came from small rural areas were they could keep their front and back doors unlocked. Now they were in a place were you had to keep both doors locked? They came from areas were the locals all knew each other, and yes every now and then you would hear of some ole boy getting shot chasing someone else's gal. Then you would hear of some ole boy getting hung by the Klan. But life in the big city was far different; a man could go to work early in the morning come home and think nothing happened in his house. Now, every now in then the local Cop or the landlord would be seen sneaking out of someone's house. The colored children now went to colored schools taught by colored school teachers.

You had colored Lawyers and Doctors and now they had what they called Auxiliary policemen, colored men that were hired by the city to keep a watch on the colored people most of them were Masons or returning veterans that got these jobs. You had fire clubs that were black, and you had the policy makers (numbers).

34

While life for Sarah was changing as well and Big Cliff was in more things than he could handle. Now as a father and husband he had real responsibilities and he also had an outside daughter to care for.

Now my Grandma Gurtie, with only a six grade education, which was given to her from her own cousin in Virginia kept her husbands book straight, straighter than if he had a real Accountant.

Now at the same time down in Little Italy the Local Don was not at all happy that Ole Cliff made that trip to Chi town. Number one he wasn't going to let no colored boy, as he called Cliff, be up staged by him in front of a young under Boss like Frank Netty. Nor was he taking orders from a young up and coming Don like Al Capone. So this would have been the making of a small war in SoBo. If it wasn't for the quick thinking of Big Cliff's Uncle Isiah!

What he did was go down there himself to cut a deal with that Family that controlled SoBo.

He told that Don that he would see that Cliff would never do that again and that he would not let his railroad men get involved with this. He would see that the new rail line that his crews were working on in Sparrows Point would use his trucks to load the gravel and raw materials that the Railroad needed. Since he had a Gold Watch from the President of the B and O Railroad he had the inside connection!

The Ole Don was impressed by this six foot plus black man, so much that he invited Uncle Isiah down to Little Italy to drink some wine and have a real Italian dinner with him. They also watched a film on Jack Johnson's last fight. "Hey'a you, a good boy." said that Ole Don to great Uncle Isiah. "I know you got some big boys working on them a rail.

Can any of them boys you a got fight?"

Well, Uncle Isiah wasn't anybodies fool, so he sent Uncle Zep down there to find out was that Ole guy going to keep his word.

He didn't want any of Big Cliff's boys going down there and shooting up the place so he told Zep to keep it quiet.

Well sure to his word the I-Talin Don kept his hot heads from coming up town and starting a war with Granddaddies boys.

Uncle Isiah had Cliff and his boys go down to Ann Arundal County to scout out some land for a new road house close to Route 3.

He told him that if he went alone that the Klan might get him and he would be the next nigger they hung. Well, Granddaddy wasn't a Hero so he got Uncle Jimi and a few of his boys to go with him. Uncle Isiah knew that by the time Cliff and the boys got back to Baltimore that everything would be in place and the war would not happen.

Great Uncle Isiah had to call in every favor he had to keep the West side from exploding that summer of 1920.

Not only that, he now had a good friend in that Don, once he brought him that big ole boy that could lay more tracks than anyone and could knock out any three of Uncle Isiah's work crews. They called that ole boy Tom, Big Tom McClain.

That Ole boy, Tom McClain, could fight, but he didn't know how to fight. Them I-Talians took that ole boy and trained him in a gym down there in Little Italy with other white fighters, any of them white fighters that didn't want to fight or train next to a colored fighter. Well we will just say that they no longer fought in that gym. All I know at this point is that that Don had big plans for his Baltimore family and that fighter was going to be the opener to that can he wanted open!

Now that Uncle Isiah got the I-Talians cool and Mr. Frank Netty was happy with the way things were being run in Little Italy. He also got a big cut in the Cuban operation and a small part of the action in any fights that Big Tom McClain fought. He left a small group of his boys in SoBo to start the policy operation down there and to keep an eye on that Ole Baltimore Don.

Well, to some of you reading this it might seem that policy and crime and things connected to them was all that got people through. But, let me say that it was people helping other people that got people through life the best way they could. Without my Grandfather's act of honesty and integrity, he would have never met or been involved with the families in Little Italy. Without the involvement of my Great Grandmother with a Jewish lawyer many colored people would not have a chance in the legal world of 1920. It's all about people and their reactions with other people that God keeps this ole world running and not falling completely through or in the hands of the evil one.

"Morning" "Good morning" said Gail to Sarah. "Well gal how are you?"

"I just don't know gal." said Sarah back. "I'm kind of confused right about now. My mama wants me to raise little Cliff and keep him away from his daddies bar, and I love going to them social things that I go too with the Bernstein's family. But I just don't know about me and Jack these days? I been thinking hard on them things lately gal. I can't keep my mind on my business any more like I use too."

"Well, good." said Gail, "we will start within a few days to go up town to them rich white folks home. It's a good trade and there is a need for more hair-dressers. You can let Hattie and Zep run your grocery stores and the lunch room and let Gurtie collect your rents. If you keep doing what you doing no body will be happy so you and me gal we are going to start living and that little baby will be just ok with us in the shop. And as far as Jack is concerned what he doesn't know want hurt him. Gal, we going up town and fool some Jews and white woman in believing that we can make them look like movie stars."

Chapter 7

"You must not look better than those white women, so wear your pretty black hair in a tigron when you go into their homes. They do not enjoy being waited upon by a quadroon who has more beautiful hair than their own."

Gail who was brown skin and had the average colored woman's hair often had to wear this scarf to keep her hair down and had to use lots of grease to make it lay flat and Madame Walker's hot comb. She would help Sarah with her tigron, and it was very bright and lovely. Many of them were of brilliant colors –red and green, red and white, green and black, most of them were cotton, although when they got really established in their work they wore silk.

The colored ladies and the Jewish woman would come to her house in the basement beauty salon that they established.

Sarah had her head bound in gold hoops and large gold ear rings; she also started to wear jewelry. But when she was with Jack she was just the plain Sarah that he came to love not the up and coming lady about town. When she was at the Theaters, up town in colored ones or downtown white ones she was the shinning star. They called her Queen Sarah then and she was the center of all attention.

Sarah was finding out that she was even more remarkable in appearance now. Watching her put her tigron on, Gail smiled. The tigron (scarf) was a trick of our woman- an old trick. "It makes the white people feel more comfortable for some reason when they see us wear them, yet they make us look better than ever."

Sarah also started to wear make up, she veiled her eyes with her long black lashes and raised her head arrogantly.

"We must please the white woman, I suppose." she said, curling her upper lip a little. "We are not there to steal their husbands." laughed Gail, "but to make some money and if their husbands want some on the side I do their hair also!" laughed Gail.

"Gal, you have no shame do you?"

"Nope!" said Gail. "Broke pockets and hungry stomachs makes this gal from New Orleans go crazy." said Gail.

"Do you think that this scarf over my hair will make them white women not be jealous of me?" said Sarah.

Gail was now beside herself in laughter.

"The way you look, it might not work. Don't wear a tight dress, wear one of them house dresses with an apron in front of it. We must also act a little stupid too and miscount our money also; it makes them feel good when they give us a tip!

At the same time that Sarah was becoming a Queen, my Grandmother Gurtie; (Sarah's oldest daughter) was becoming a great businesswoman, straightening out the books for my Granddaddy which was a job and a half. The accounts were all wrong and the recipes that he gave her were wrong, and the tally on the beer was always off and there were many problems that she began to address. My father who was now turning one year old was staying up on McCullah Street, being spoiled by all those hairdressers that my Great-grandmother had working in the basement.

Although Gurtie was a short woman she was a Tolson through and through and with a temper that matched her father. She was not like her mother in no way and she was manlier in her make up than her mother who was head and shoulders taller than her.

I once saw a picture of Grandmother at a Halloween party dressed up as a man I couldn't believe how much she could pass as a very handsome man!

Not only was my grandmother a go getter she took complete control of the business end of all my Grandfathers businesses. He was more or less free to enjoy his time in the country with his buddies.

My Grandmother had to remove some of the family that were thinking that it was ok to take a little here and a little there. She not only moved them but brought more members into the different places that needed help the most the most important one was on Route one.

The main thing that that place needed the most was a good cook. So the lunch room cook was sent to the country not without a fuss.

"Now I been working for Cliff now for three or four years" said Miss Annabelle "and I'm not going to just pick myself up and move to no country! I left the country to come here and I loves living in SoBo. I'm going to stay" she said.

"Now look sweetheart I'm not telling you to stop working for Cliff, he needs someone with your special skills out there to take over things and to run them right." said Gurtie to Miss Annabelle.

You see my Grandmother had a way of making people feel very important and she never, ever raised her voice not once to any one.

Now my Granddaddy needed Jimi to back him up and he needed Uncle Isiah to think clearly for him. But Grandma Gurtie could do it all by herself.

There was nothing she could not do and when it came time for her to work, well she would be the first one there on time.

She had all the Laws girls working and dressing better at the lunch room. She had the Monroe girls working where ever they were needed since there were seven of them; she made sure that they were all getting paid running up and down Route 301 or U.S. one.

Now this was a big help to Big Cliff, he had about thirteen of the best looking brown skin gal's working for him and seven of them were his half- sisters and five were his cousins and one his sister-in-Law.

One ole boy told him, "Man, you could take them Gal's up to New York City, to the Cotton Club and replace that whole chorus line!" laughing as he was talking. Man that's how it was in the early twenties in ole Baltimore.

Sarah said "Must I act deaf, blind and stupid!" "Promise me Sarah that you won't lose that Indian temper of yours and kill some poor ole white woman. Ok?" said Gail.

"I will try girl but you know how I feel about that "N" word it burns me up. All I can remember was how ole Tolson would call my children little "N" cause they all weren't light skin like his other kids!" said Sarah. "But I think I will be all right, you know I think that they think we can't hear or see or use our mind and I think that they feel we don't have feelings." said Gail

They both sank on the edge of Sarah's new bed laughing, in her new bedroom that was bigger than her old house. It had closets in it, a sitting area, plus a reading area and three bowed windows that faced the front of the street all the way around to the next cross street.

"It will pay off in the long run gal, if we just follow their orders because, gal once they see us as human beings we are out. All we will do is follow orders, and say, 'Yes Madame and No Madame", I think we put a little French on them to throw them off some, ok?" said Sarah.

"You can laugh inside, but not out loud, and we can't talk back to any of them, if we want to work for them a second time. Those new immigrants, them Irish people are trying to take all the jobs we use to do.

Of course I don't mean to say we can't meet some times and talk about them, but after we finish our jobs!" said Gail to Sarah.

"Most of them that I have met are very nice, that's because of the way that I been acting but you never can let your guard down around them." said Gail.

"But dear we will learn a lot from them and make a lot of money. You just watch me for awhile and you will see how it's done. They will, after a while tell you of all their troubles, and a lot more. They think that we don't really pay any attention. But we can use what they say, later when it counts. It's almost like they were talking to themselves." said Gail.

So Sarah and Gail set out to begin their journey with the rich and famous of North Baltimore.

Meanwhile down on Druid Hill and Orchard Street, one of her children was following in her foot steps.

Grandma Gurtie was becoming the same type of a person as her mother but she had her father's ways and hang-ups. She just took over things, running everything and she was a born leader, she had all the ole men acting better and the young men dressing better. She would cook for each of them and make them think that it was just for them that she was doing it for. She would say, 'Hey Robert, come around early and I'll fry you some chicken', or make some pork crops for old Uncle Al the way he wanted them and fish she took everything that Cliff did down in her mind.

She would visit someone first and never stop asking about this one or that one. Her cousin's were like sisters to her, each one was special to her, not one member of the Laws or Tolson family went without her stopping by or the Monroe's and the Chase and Seeney family as while.

If any one needed any thing she was there fast with what ever they needed, her sisters were like jewelry to her what she had they had also.

There was no fighting or Tom foolery around her and she went up on Orchard Street to the A.M.E church every Sunday morning.

Now Cliff and the boys were out in the country building that new road house, and one thing he liked more than anything was swimming. So, they would all get together and go any time that the weather was nice. Everyone in the family would load up and make a day down on the bay listening to the latest music and musicians that were in town because Robert Monroe Junior knew all of them.

Now ole bow legs was still hustling with his pony boys down in SoBo (South Baltimore) and now that there were so many new people up in West Baltimore he expanded his business to include trash pick up. You see the city had a kind of trash pick up, but it was mostly for down town Baltimore and white areas.

He was the kind of person that could fill any void that the city left open and along with his Army of pony boys called A-rabs he was able to have work for the less fortunate black men of the city.

The new arrivals could get a job as helpers on the junk wagons and if they didn't drink or chase the road side gal's they could save up there pennies and rent a fruit wagon which was the top of the A-rabs life.

Now this is how they would pick up the trash that they collected early in the morning by yelling "trash pick up, bring out your trash, fifteen cents a pick up." They would haul the trash out to a dump somewhere in the country, own by some farmer and dump it down his hill and try to beat each other back to the city to get more.

You see Ole Uncle Robert would rent the wagons to them boys at ten cents a day and charge ten cents for the ponies that he bought from the same farmer that had the land fill. So the more them boys picked up the more money Ole Uncle Robert and his partners, the Queen family made.

Now those Queens were still in the junk business in Halthrope when I was growing up fifty years later.

Well what they did was they have these large barns set up in SoBo for them boys to work out of.

My Ole Uncle had a dream and a little money but Ole man Queen had the barns that his white daddy left him so it was only natural that the two would get together and use some of the family money to get the junk business off the ground.

Now like everything that a colored man did a white man had to have a law against it, to try to take control of it. So the city, forced them to get a licenses to pick up trash!

Now that little piece of paper had to be on every wagon and at a dollar a license, Ole Rob was beside himself.

"Hey Rob" said Jimi, "why don't you go and see Miss Sarah and get her help on them city licenses." "Yea man, good idea!" said Rob to Jimi.

Rob knew she would be home on Mondays so that Grandma could pick up my daddy. "Hey, Miss Sarah I needs your help bad." he said.

Zep and Gurtie

Chapter 8

Most of Sarah's new clients she found pleasant enough. There was the occasional harridan who screeched at her crossly, and several who tried to talk her into cutting her fee especially for them. These were the ones that she was personally going to stop herself.

Several times a week she and Gail would go up to the New Druid Hill Park area, around Brookfield Ave. to do the wealthy white women's hair and then over to the Mount Royal area to do the rich Jewish women's hair. There where fine houses along Mount Royal, mansions lining Brookfield Ave. and there were fine townhouses on Madison and the main street Whitlock Ave.

Sarah grew very skillful with the long and straight white women's hair and the wavy and curly and often times the kinky Jewish women's hair. Sometimes she had hair that was as tight as colored woman's hair and then she had the ones that hair was to fine to set, which would just lay flat on their heads. She found no different in colored people's hair and white, the only thing was the degree of curl.

She grew skilled in arranging curls and braids and buns, in curling hair that was straight, in straightening hair that was too curly and she delighted in the fact that many of her clients had colored blood.

There were ladies who required the artful use of transformations, false curls and hairpieces. There was one, a very heavy middle aged beauty who had to wear a full wing on her head at plays, the theater and at balls. There were others who were graying and their tresses had to be dyed and tainted, she would use special things that Gail had to make, strong black dyes like black day old coffee, charcoal sticks, blueberry juice and blackberry juice.

During her training she would listen very closely to how Gail would let the clients talk, she would seldom talk herself, only if the person asked her. She would move quietly through the houses and in the boudoirs. Her manners were improving and she was fast becoming less outspoken with her family and friends and especially with Jack.

She was slowly becoming a lady which her daughters picked up and especially my Grandma Gurtie. The social season was fast approaching that would start around Easter and end New Years day of 1921.

There would be the theater and the night in the Park, and great Operas, there were balls and fancy soirees. And as the weeks past they together picked up many new clients.

The word would spread like so 'I hear that Mrs. Van Pelt on Madison has a new colored hairdresser, oh do tell, how is Mrs. Agnes Van Pelt looking these days! She's looking ten years younger and much slimmer as well!'

The next day Mrs. Van Pelt would get a call 'Hello dear can you send that colored hairdresser who is making you look so fantastic around to me when you have some time. I hear she does the hair of that famous Opera star Miss. so and so!'

Most of the rich white women were in a frantic mood; their engagements were so many that each had to be better than their friends and most had to have their hair done more than once a week. Yes, there were many other hairdressers in town, both black and white of course, but Madame Gail and her partner as they were now called, were in great demand by many of the wealthiest ones.

It got so good that if you needed them to do your hair you had to make the trip down to the 1000 block of McCullah Street, were you had to make and appointment with them first.

They would only do hair Tuesdays and Thursday's now. As the summer got hotter there were less and less appointments.

A certain lady was married to one of the men on the city counsel, a Mrs. Forshaw, whose husband was a very important member of the city government. Well, she had a very tender scalp and she couldn't brush her own hair and none of the other hairdressers would take her. But Sarah did, because Hattie had the same problem. It was the very soft touch of Sarah's hands and her soft song that Mrs. Forshaw enjoyed so much. So much so that every night she would have her driver drive to Sarah's house to get her long hair brushed. And she would be at peace sitting there getting her hair brushed, it was one of those nights that Sarah broke her song and said something to the Lady. "Miss Forshaw, my son-in-laws brother is having a problem with the new hauling licenses that the city has which has made my trash man pay also. I just don't know what I'm going to do if he stops, I might have to move away from this nice house to be near the county were they don't pay for the license. Can you ask your husband to help me please?"

In no time at all, the hauling license was reduced to a dollar a year and only the owner of the wagon had to have it.

Now, that got many of them ole white guys down there in pig town mad as hell, because they were doing the same thing without one and the pig town police only picked on the colored wagons.

Now the A- rabs could travel all over the city and show the cops if they were stopped a paper that the owner of the wagon gave them. This paper was proof that the owner of the wagon was licensed to do what they were doing. The paper would say wagon owned by so and so and a phone number that the cop could call from his call box. This got to be too much trouble for the cops, so they quit stopping those A- rabs! Later it would be a copper plate that was nailed to the back of the wagons.

For almost every moment of her waking hours she was thinking of Jack, remembering him like the next day would be their last day.

She saw Mr. Bernstein, often and spent long hours talking to him, learning more and more about him and the city and the legal world that he was involved in.

He would go on and on talking about this case or that case and the in's and the out's and how he was going to handle them. He taught her so much over that summer of 1920 she felt that she could go down town and settle a law suit if she had to.

She knew that he was a lonely man and she knew that all his wife cared about was their children and her social standing in the Jewish community.

She felt bold enough one day to ask him if he and his wife were having sex, just like that!

He looked at her the same way and told her that he didn't!

"Well, that explains a lot to me." she said.

"Well, you see after she had our last child see was to hurt inside of her womb to ever have sex, so we have learned all these years to go without it." he said. "Does it bother you that I look at you with desire?" he said "No," she replied "I thought that you were in need for a woman" she said.

'No, if I needed a woman I would do just like so many others do and there are many girls on the streets nowadays selling themselves. I need a special person, one that I can do more than just make love to or should I say have sex with." He said "I want and need a friend first and then someone who wants me, just as I am!"

"Oh, that's very faltering if you are referring to me." she said. Well, what are we going to do about how you feel?" she said to him.

"Well I don't know about you but I would love to feel you all over me!" he said. Trying to be as passionate as he knew how he said "let's make a special date for this." To her surprise, "I think that would be wonderful." she replied back.

"We could go out to the country and make a picnic out of it," she said. "I will fry some chicken and make some potato salad and some other things." she said". Just then a funny feeling went all over her body and she began to feel her heart broke. She knew that this was the first time that she would ever have sex outside of Jack and it was breaking her heart to know that she was willing to break this.

Oh Jack, she thought I do love you. I would never think of hurting you, she thought to herself.

"Maybe we should wait dear till I feel the same for you." she said to him.

"I see I know that I was rushing you I will wait till you are ready and I know that, that Day will come soon." he said.

She has never met such a understanding man in her life and she was feeling torn between the two loves in her life. Never in her wildest dreams would she believe that two white men were in love with her at the same time.

For a long time Sarah was disappointed that she was not hearing some astounding and interesting gossip from her clients. It was true the women talked, both to her and to friends who might be present while she worked, but at first she found it difficult to concentrate upon it and her profession at the same time. Later, as her work became increasingly automatic, she became more conscious of their chatter, but none of it seemed of any consequence.

The most vicious might concern the love affair of a friend's husband, the "truth" about the cause of some fight or other, or the expected bankruptcy of some acquaintance.

After a while Sarah, ceased paying much attention to this and decided that after all Gail was getting old and gossipy herself, and lonely, too, and so probably a bit given to exaggeration.

Most of the women coming to get their hair done in the fall of 1920 were not as interesting as they were before in the spring of the year.

It was on an afternoon when she was doing Mrs. Forshaw hair that any thing interesting was said. A new lady to her establishment by the name of Jean Fortney came in. Who was a tall thin woman with a long, proud throat and the face of a bird, with immense eyes, large, hooked nose and almost no chin? Her hair was dark blonde, fine as silk, but as thin as the rest of her, and she added to the elaborate coiffure, she preferred several false pieces and clusters of curls attached on combs at her temples, which fell to her shoulders.

They fill out my face she explained to Sarah. She was vain, but she was what Gail called "a nice person," and she was nice to Sarah. She was patient, quick with compliments when she was especially pleased, and generous of both money and spirit. Her husband owned a down town brewery.

It seemed to Sarah that Mrs. Forshaw spent all her time down town at the hotels on Charles Street getting room service and socializing. But her younger daughter Della was left alone a lot.

What seemed strange to Sarah while doing Mrs. Forshaw hair, she had a vision and in that vision she saw Jack he was getting married and that woman that he was marring wasn't her.

In her mind she saw him, and it was exactly like the terrible dreams she had before. There he was with another a white woman, his eyes were closed, and his face was like marble. Sarah gasped and her hands tightened, Gail who was near shrieked and leaped to her feet, a frantic arm sweeping Sarah to one side. A drop of blood drop from Mrs. Forshaw hair and down to her cheek.

Sarah was just standing there looking at her, as if she was looking at a ghost. Then the picture of the wedding faded and was gone. There was only Gail standing holding her and Mrs. Forshaw with blood on her face.

"Are you ill"?

"Yes" whispered Sarah.

"Sit down dear! Please sit down." Mrs. Forshaw said to her as tenderly as ones own mother would say. Gail took her up stairs to her bedroom and put her under some covers while Mrs. Forshaw brought her some tea that was very hot from her large kitchen.

Mrs. Forshaw put a finger in the wet spot on her cheek while Mrs. Fortney brought her a towel.

"Heavens!" I'm so very sorry!" Sarah cried out to all in her bedroom. Sinking deeper into her feather bed, a gentle hand pressed her forehead.

"It doesn't matter dear." said Mrs. Forshaw to her Gail was rattling her drawers looking for her salts!

"Girl you fainted" said Gail to her. "I'll be all right Sarah."

"I can never find anything when I want to!" fumed Gail. Slamming shut a drawer and forsaking her search for her smelling salts. Rushing back to the bed with a bottle of perfume in her hand, "Smell this child" Gail said to Sarah.

"It may help her I'll get you some brandy or some wine if you have any." said Mrs. Fortney.

"Are any of your children here that can help us?" she said to Sarah.

"I don't know maybe." Sarah said to her.

As Mrs. Fortney rushed to the downstairs she ran into what she thought was the handsomest man she ever saw he had black straight hair and a great smile on his broad face, he was tall much taller than the men she was use to, he was her size. He was well built and very muscular, his complexion was a light golden hue just then she woke from her encounter.

"Is there something wrong here?" the voice was of an angle to her.

"Oh! Yes." Mrs. Fortney said "Your mother, she is your mother young man isn't she?"

"Yes" Zep said, "What's wrong?"

"Oh, she had a vision or a daydream and she fainted." "I know of them I have them myself." Zep said, "let me see if I can help her."

"What are you going to do?" she enquired of him. "I'm going to get some incense that my grandmother brought up here to help her sleep."

"Ok" she said, "let's hurry then." following him to a downstairs room that he used as his own small apartment. Zep got the incense and hurried to his mother's side lighting them. The smell was too much for the other women they had to leave the room to return to the living room waiting for Zep to bring them good news. Just as they were setting down Hattie and Mary came in and ran to their mother's room they too could not stand the smell and had to retreat to the living room.

"She will be ok in a day or so." Zep said to all of them. "We have these visions when something is on our mind and troubling us. My sisters are of the blood of our father, they don't have such things it is me and my sisters that have the blood of our father that have these visions and dreams."

A day later Gail returned to Sarah's house to open the salon and to check on Sarah. She was coming back to her bed when Gail came into the room the smelled the incense was gone and she was trying to regain her strength.

"Hi, gal are you feeling better?" a look of suspicion was on her face. Sarah had no trouble reading her mind.

"You're not …?"

"No," said Sarah bluntly, the irony of that suggestion was giving her a fresh shock.

"I'll get along now."

"I saw him!" Sarah said "he was getting married"!

"Oh, my child, I thought something was happening to you." Gail said.

Gail scarcely knew what she was saying.

"Who was getting married baby?"

Sarah big eyes softened with her friend's sympathy. "Oh, I'm so sorry." Sarah said.

"When did it happen?" Gail tried to put it together.

"I don't know," Sarah said to her." I don't know yet".

Mary entered the room "Ain't you a big gal now!" Gail said to her as she carried some brandy to her mother.

"Would you care for some Miss Gail" Mary said to her.

"My, my, aren't we getting classy up in here now." Gail said to her.

When Mary left the room Gail said "I'm going to send you away to get away from these white men, they are driving you crazy gal. I'm going to buy you a ticket to sail to my home and get some real sun and fresh air. It will do you good gal, you been working to hard here and these men are tearing you apart.

But, I don't understand it, the day before yesterday you seemed perfectly ok when I arrived at the salon, and after Mrs. Forshaw, came you were ok. Was it, Mrs. Fortney?"

"All I know was when I was doing Mrs. Forshaw, I had that vision." said Sarah.

"It is wrong to hold anything like that in; you should not have come today." said Gail.

"I didn't know it then." Sarah said to Gail.

"Only a moment after I touched her hair I saw it and I couldn't handle it!" she said.

"Child that sounds like you touched more then her hair, I think you touched her soul and there is something deep and dark in there."

"Forgive me Gail I just don't know, it is just something I saw."

Gail stared and her gaze covered Sarah, from head to foot, and returned to her face. "I see." she said slowly.

She paused and took a deep breath.

Then she smiled faintly.

"I'll go and see about that ticket for you. I want you to go to my home in New Orleans and live a little and I'm not going to take no for an answer!" Gail said.

For a week in September Sarah went south, as far south as you can go and still be in the United States. No one knew except Gail, not even her children knew were she was.

Sarah was not having a regular vacation like most people have but she was in a strange and beautiful world, a world of new sounds and new colors, new people and new customs, which would have people in Baltimore calling her a witch if they knew.

She met Gail's mother and children and her husband. She was so surprised that Gail had such a large family there and a husband.

Sarah ate with them and listened to them explain why Gail was not with them and why she was so far from them. They told her that an evil woman put roots on Gail for her husband when she was young and no matter what she did she was unhappy here.

The farther she got from all of them the happier she got. To Sarah that was so sad, but she began to understand.

One day walking down Decatur Street with one of Gail's daughters she was stopped by a certain man, he introduced himself to her as Captain Christopher Sharp, he said that he watched her as she crossed the wide Boulevard from Congo Square to Decatur Street. And that he felt that he had to introduce himself to her.

He was a nice size man; thin with curly black hair he said that he was a sea Captain on a ship from Santo Domingo to New Orleans.

"Miss, I mean no disrespect to you or your daughter, but I had to speak to you. You Madame are the picture of sunshine." he said to her.

"Well thank you and this isn't my daughter, my daughters live in Baltimore, Maryland." she replied to him.

"Oh just my luck you live thousands of miles from my heart." he said to her.

"Sir, you make such a bold remark to me, and you just met me." she replied back to him.

"Yes Madame, I did, pardon moi." he said in French. "I didn't mean to say anything that might upset you. But, I wanted to find out your name!"

"Oh, is that all, my name is Sarah."

"Glade to meet you Sarah." he said. "Do you live here in New Orleans?"

"No, I'm just visiting my friend's family for a few weeks, and then I'm returning back to Baltimore."

"Oh I'm so sorry about that; maybe I can stop and pay you a visit?" he said to her while holding her hand.

"Maybe you can?" she said.

"That would be nice, and we might have a drink and go to a play in the French quarters." he said. "Where can I call on you my flower?"

"Oh, you are a charmer aren't you!" she said.

"Nay ma Mon amant I'm just a hopeless romantic." he replied.

Uncle Isiah and my Grandfather Big Cliff on the right

Chapter 9

Her little romantic encounter lasted for the time that she stayed in New Orleans and it then it was back to Baltimore. She was sailing back home on one of the Cuban ships that were friends of Big Cliff's.

She wrote Gurtie, and told her where she was and that she needed her to get her a way back home. At once Grandma Gurtie was on it, she told the whole family that her mother was taking a vacation, and that she was tired and needed the time to herself.

She told Cliff that she needed him to get her a first class ticket on one of his friend's boats that was anchored down in Curtis bay. The ticket was not to be made know to any one.

This was the instructions that her mother sent her. The only one that knew that she was so far away was Gail who sent her there and Grandmother, why was this such a secret I have no idea.

But it did free my great Grandmother's mind from the problems that she was having up to that time.

On board the ship back, the Captain of the boat asked her was her small cabin comfortable and was there any thing that he could do to make the long trip to Baltimore any more comfortable.

She told him that it would do till she was safe at home and that she didn't want the crew of the ship making any special things for her or going out their way for her.

"Treat me as one of the family!" she laughed at the Capitain! "Si, I will." replied the Captain back at her.

That made the voyage back to Baltimore a pleasant one.

Gail found a handkerchief and blew her nose. "I guess I'll go over to the bar and get me some good beer from ole Cliff. I haven't seen him lately; hear tell he sends all his time down in the country. I bet he got himself a little filly down there! I'm not at all in the least bit ashamed of what I do. That man got a real good looking half-brother I'd like to throw my legs around, mmm, that tall brown man. I hear he's got all them gals up on Druid Hill Ave. running crazy. I bet I got something that would slow him down. Once I get through with him he be just like a child at Christmas with a new toy. I know I'm just something else with my new hair style and these high heel shoes, them ole country boys have never seen it pock out so far and this breast holder makes my baby bottles stand up. Gal's you better watch out Ole Gail is stepping out tonight."

Well it was Friday night at Cliff's, the people were saying it's going to be a Indian summer. The weather was just right. Cliff's like every little joint had a piano player and a Jazz singer.

The beer was flowing and the people were coming in, happy that the weekend was here. Cliff and Gurtie were behind the bar they had to hire a weekend waitress by the name of Bessie, she was a high yellow gal that the men that came in the bar really enjoyed. In the front was big Shirley cooking fried chicken wings and shad and lake trout. Standing by the front door sitting sometimes was big Jake.

Hazel would be waiting the tables and most times it was standing room only and the few tables were always full, the bar would also carry over into the back court yard that they used when the weather was nice.

Out in the alley there would be the usual dice game. Jimi and ole Robert would be up to their old bag of tricks. But most times the fellows in the game knew them so it was pretty honest.

Now and then someone who wasn't from the area would try to make a reputation in the alley only to end up in City Hospital or worse in the harbor, down at pier 6 and a half.

The road side gal's didn't come around there because of Grandma who would run them away. Uncle Ed and Great Uncle Al would pop in every now and then when they weren't up at the new Masonic hall.

Cliff would get, every now in then, his people together and head down to the country and they would have a caravan every now and then that started to be once a month.

"Man, I can remember when we used to be up in here with just old second hand clothes that we bought down at that ole Jewish man shop in SoBo."

"Yea," said Cliff. "Remember when I got out of the Navy, the first place I headed to was that ole greasy spoon down on Hamburger Street in Pig town to get me some of them white folks polish dogs."

"Yea man" said Jimi. "I just couldn't see myself going over there. You boys sure had some balls going to war for them white folks.'

"No man" said Cliff, "it was for us that we went over there."

"Well" said Jimi, "you didn't do much fighting did you!"

"No" said Cliff, "but man, them German subs were all over the place, a couple of my shipmates in the galley were hit off of France in 17."

"Man, you never told me that!"

"Yea man" said Cliff "it wasn't like you think. We had to hunt those subs like a hunter hunts deer.

Man we had to sit out there and wait for them German sub boats to come up for air before we went after them to sink them. I did more then just cook all the time, man, I had to load them trash cans with T.N.T…"

"What's that?" said Cousin Rob Tolson.

'Man. that's the most unstable dynamite there is." said Cliff.

"I hear tell that you are in one of them Auxiliaries down town."

"Yea man, I got sent to one because they like my cooking so much and because I'm a Chief Petty Officer."

"Well, well, an officer in the family."

"Yea man!" as they all laughed at each other, passing a bottle of beer around.

"Hey, Cliff them ole I-talians still giving you the blues."

"No man, after me, Jimi, and Zep."

"Where did he get too any way?"

"Like I was saying after me, Jimi and young Zep went up to the windy city to talk to ole Al they started working with us, 'now I don't want none of you big mouth niggers starting any trouble up here.' I got them ole boys to quiet down now, ok!" said Cliff

"Man he must be drunk, his Uncle got them I-talians to quiet down!" said one of the fellows to the guy standing next to him.

"Yea and I hear that the big man in Chi' town came down here too".

"No fool, you want to get your big mouth beat in by Jimi, you better hush up if you know what good for your dumb ass!" said another.

"Man I'm just glade I made enough to go out this week."

"Yea man".

"Times ain't all that good for me neither." said someone else changing the conversation".

"Yea, I had about two jobs last week, and if it wasn't for ole man Monroe, down at the chicken plant I wouldn't have got them."

"Man, let me tell you where you can get a good job." "Where!"

Then the whole group said "WHERE Man?"

"Well, Ole Cliff there Uncle is hiring men to work on that new steel mill plant that they are building down in Sparrows point".

"Yea, man I hear all you got to do is be out there on Mulberry Street, with a lunch pale in your hand at 4:30 in the morning and the wagon will pick you up and take you down there".

"Man I needs me some money and a job."

"Yea, man I needs to work more then two or three days a week!"

"Man, I hear tell them boys are working every day and Sunday too and you can make a dollar a day!"

"That sounds good to me; my rent is fifty cents a month."

"Boy, oh boy, the good times have come back to B-More."

"Yea, it beats working down in Pig town with them pigs, and them white boys don't want us down there any ways".

"Man, I'm not drinking any more I'm going to get myself home to my ole lady and tell her the news!"

"Hey, James Royal, you coming?"

"Sarah, the other day when you told me about your dream, I was thinking about what happen to me in New Orleans when I first got married. You met him when you were there." said Gail to Sarah.

"He's a very fine looking dark man." said Sarah

"Yes he is and when I first met him he was a lot bigger in the body. Now that he has age on him he's getting thinner." said Gail. "Well we got married when we were young I was a city girl and he was a country boy working on a barge. I just couldn't help falling in love with that big black boy and them arms that were so big. He got them big arms from lifting those bails of cotton from that barge to the pier all day built him up. Well honey it was love at first sight. We got married as soon as I could to Nick. After we started having babies he had to find different kind of work and down there you were a field hand or a house nigger, oh, Sarah I'm sorry about that word!" she said.

"Well he wasn't one to work in the house and he had no skills to do anything else. You see I got me a job working as a hairdresser down there. So he was left taking care of our little shack on Ann Street and the chillings (Children). Now next door to us was this fat old woman and her daughters, they were as black as the night and hair that looked like steel wool. Now that fat ole so and so had about ten chilling, all by different men. She got money the best way she could, stealing and telling white people fortunes. Yes, she was a root woman, and she put a mojo on me to get my man. So after a while we would just fight and fuss all the time and ole Nick stared drinking a lot. Where he got the money I soon found out. She had him doing the stealing for her, and paying him in cheap rum. I just couldn't take any more so I left my chilling and husband there and moved where the money was, till I ended up here in Baltimore staying at your boarding house.

Now once I was here for a while the blues left me and that Mojo was broken. That's why I sent you far from here and far from your family and friends and them men, to break that Mojo that someone put on you."

"Well." Sarah said "That's about a mouth full you were telling me. I do fill a lot different and happier and my dreams have changed as well. I don't dream or see Jack in them anymore, and my feelings for him aren't over powering me any more, did I tell you I met a man?"

"Where gal?"

"In your home, he was from that Island where these people on that block I used to live on were from."

"Do tell me more gal." said Gail to Sarah laughing.

At this time it was Grandma's favorite time of the year preserving and wine making, the crop was in and harvest time was here.

"Sure glade we didn't have any trouble tonight baby."

"How much money did we tack in tonight, babe?" Grandma told Grandpa, "Well after we take the pay off and the overhead we made about a thousand dollars this week."

"Well girl it pays to have music in here and opening the back up, we can get more people in here.

That sounds like a real nice weekend to me, yea, and on Sunday all we got to do is serve chicken dinners to the Church folks that will be in here after Church.

Now, you make sure that you clean every thing up and use plenty of pine oil and Murray's soap to get them sprits smell out of here. Ham Bone get Jake and Mildred to help you work all night, now see you boys in the morning. Now Mildred don't keep them boys from doing their work." Grandma told them.

The next morning before the rosters could crow Grandma was down in the Bar with more soap and pine oil to make sure the smell was out. She would be opening all the windows and the doors; she had the place pretty well aired out.

Now, when I was a little older I remembered that the bar had regular windows and not that big front store windows and it had fans way up in the ceilings that were giant size, I think their were six of them running all the way back to the kitchen.

Well any way, the place took on a new appearance, from Friday night and Saturday. It was Sunday morning and the dinners smelled up the whole bottom, that's what they called Druid Hill and Orchard Street then.

Once Grandma made sure everything was ready she went down to the Church, the same one ole Harriet Tubman use to get the slaves up north. Granddaddy was in bed resting getting ready to go to the National Guard Armory on Howard Street to get the morning chow ready. You see he was still in the reserves as a Chief Petty Officer, in the Navy.

Now, the best thing that my Grandma could make outside of Granddaddies fish and other things that she quickly picked up was her cherry wine made out of wild cherries. Let me tell you nothing in God's good Earth could taste as sweet. If you weren't a wine drinker, you would become one if you drank too much of her cherry wine. Now the boys were always coming around, eating up all Granddaddies food and massing with the gal's while he was in the country or doing his Reserve duties.

Grandma had to get control of the situation and command respect from that group of Granddaddies pals.

Life was different when you always have ten to twenty people always underfoot.

Much of the time Grandma didn't have time to go to the rest room, let alone take care of a baby. So much of the time Little Mary was the babysitter, who always took care of her little papoose, even when he was grown up.

One day a customer came to the parlor that was very rich and said that she was a friend of Mrs. Forshaw.

62

The lady stood still for moment, holding the basement door ajar. Then she suddenly closed it. "Sarah Green, is that your name?" as a good looking colored man dressed in a chauffeur's uniform brought her belongings into the shop and set them on a settee that was in the lounge.

"Yes, I'm her." said Sarah to the lady. "May I help you today?" Startled at the change in the woman's expression!

"Sarah, I have heard that you and your partner are not only good at doing hair but you have healed a lot of people during the last flu season".

"No, Madam" said Sarah, "I healed no one!"

"But I have heard that you cured many!" said the woman

"No Madam, I cured no one." said Sarah, "I just gave them food and herbs to help them fight off the sickness that's all."

"Ok, can you do other things? I know there are people who claim that you see visions."

The Lady went on to say that: "I know that there are people who claim they can, although I've had no experience with them.

One hears of so much of that sort of thing in the City, especially among colored people."

As she set down in the nearest seat, she then pressed both of her hands to her face.

She blurted out, "Sarah, I am in trouble! Can you help me?"

Sarah studied her for a moment, then her mind started racing, her heart started beating quickly. She thought to herself, what this strange feeling I now have that is overpowering me!

Sarah said "I can't help you for I don't know what is troubling you?"

The lady found a clean white linden handkerchief and blew her nose.

"I suppose I have to tell you now!" She said, "Or if I don't you wouldn't be able to help me? But I am so ashamed!"

The lady gave a vigorous tug at her large nose. "Sarah, the other day when I heard what happened here I almost wished I had been in your place?"

She bowed her head, and repeated, "I am so ashamed! Oh, I don't really mean it, I love Henry, but it would be easier for me to know the truth than to know that he wanted another woman! I suppose I'm a vain, selfish woman, but that's the way I feel!"

Sarah rose and made herself tall." What happened, what are you talking about?"

"I heard that you saw a vision of someone marrying your man." said the lady

"That was month's ago Madam, who told you that I saw that?"

"It was Mrs., Mrs. Fortney." the lady said

"That was true I did say that I saw the man that I was in love with then marrying someone else but I'm way over that now." said Sarah

"How did you get over such a thing please tell me, I know that he's going to marry someone else and not me I can't live with out him!" cried the lady. "I just want him to come back to me."

"I might have second sight as far as my own life is concerned, but someone else's, no, I have no such power!" said Sarah.

"I know you can bring him back to me, I felt it!" said the lady.

"Felt what!" said Gail.

"I felt a force when I came in and that force told me that she can make him come back to me." said the lady.

"What force do you think a person would have, to see into the future and what power have you ever heard of could change a man's mind about a woman?" Gail said.

"You been hearing the wrong things about us colored people if we had any power we would not be under white rule?" said one of the colored ladies in the shop!

"Madame, I can't help you get your man back but I can make you over to something that he would want and something that others would want as while. Set your self down here and let me get to work on you." said Sarah.

To her astonishment the Lady began to cry. Tears rolled out of her eyes and down her cheeks and a muffled sob broke from her lips.

After Sarah did a miracle on the ladies hair and face the woman looked like another person. Later they took her upstairs to Sarah's bedroom and in the closet were the finest dresses that any colored woman could own. The colors were like a rainbow in that large closet that you could walk in and change in as well.

The lady said to her "I had no idea that you were so rich".

"That is another thing that we are going to work on, your personality." said Sarah and Gail at the same time.

Once their work with that lady was done they were out and about. After some months had pass that good looking chauffeur showed up with a note.

The note read "Thank you all so much for giving me a new life if I can be any help please fell free to call me". Mrs. McCormack.

"Oh, we must have done something right." said Gail to Sarah as she was eying that chauffeur.

"How old do you think that boy is?" said Gail to Sarah.

"Oh, I thank he about thirty something, why don't you ask him yourself?" said Sarah to Gail.

"I will. Say young men how old are you?" asked Gail.

"I am thirty five Madame".

"Oh how nice!" Gail replied.

"Oh my God gal, you are about to get yourself in a lot of trouble!" said Sarah.

Down at the Bar, Grandma was trying to get things to slow down so that she would have more time with daddy he was growing fast and the women up at the beauty parlor were spoiling him something rotten.

The first thing Grandma did was put people on shifts, she had half of them come to work in the morning about 3:00 am. Then she had some come in at 11:00 am, and then the rest were to come in at 6:00 pm.

She now had three shifts working and then she made up the weekend shift with just Bone and Jak working Friday 3:00 am and Saturday at 3:00 am they had Sunday off.

The kitchen would open at 6:00 am and that would be manned by a cook and a waitress till 8:00 am that's when she would help out in kitchen. The cleaning up was still done by Ham Bone till 11:00 am. Now if he didn't show any mornings Grandpa had to do the cleaning, which he wasn't too happy about that? He would find somebody else to do the cleaning and pay them out of his pocket, not ever letting Grandma know what he was doing, but she always had a way of finding out things.

When Jak came in he had to help Cousin Rob with the beer and wine till 12:00 pm. Then he was off till 3:00 am if he didn't show once again Grandpa had to help in the basement with the barrels of beer and wine. Now he had to be very careful who he got to help with the beer and wine so when big Jak wasn't there Uncle Alonzo Monroe was used.

Now Big Cliff's younger brother wasn't to happy doing manual labor, but it was not all the time and at nineteen years old it was better then standing on a corner waiting to shine someone shoes.

Yea, life was great when the sun was shining but now that it was getting cold in the early winter of 1920 it was better being in a nice warm basement than in the cold wind of November.

Out of every house on the block you could smell the burning of that Black Death in people's houses called coal. It was smelly and dirty and it was cheap, cheaper then wood but in the end it would kill you.

Many people in Baltimore wouldn't use it like the rich people they used wood in their fireplaces. Now most black people had small houses and these were in

Alley street one house after the other heating each other from the coal stoves in the middle of the house.

So when the family came down stairs in the morning someone had the job of shoveling the coal from the coal bend in the basement to the stove in the dinning room.

Most times it was the man of the house getting ready to go to work around 3 am. He would load the stove up for the family before he left now that load would be all the family had all day so it would burn slow.

Now the wife would be in the small kitchen fixing the days meals where the kitchen wood pile would be enough wood to keep her busy all day.

Most times the children would be doing two things on their way to work themselves or on their way to school.

Now this all depended on the frame of mind of the father, if he cared at all he would let them go to the six grade then send them off to work some where in the area.

Now you might be thinking why the history lesson, well it leads up to one of my families stories.

Now the coal that the colored areas got, all came from the same place in South Baltimore, near Pig Town and the man that controlled that coal and the price was an English man. He had the Irishmen delivering the coal to the colored areas on time payments.

So they thought, tell ole Uncle Robert found out that the Irishmen would buy the coal from that Englishman cheap. The Irishmen then would sell it high and on time to the poor colored people. Till one of the drunken Irishmen told ole bow leg's what he was a doing.

Well just like that a light went off in Uncle Roberts's head he went to Cliff and got a ton of money to buy up all the coal he could. So he loaded up his wagons and started off early in the morning down there to Camden yards.

Once the Irishmen saw all those colored men driving wagons, coming down there to pick up the coal they blocked them with theirs and called the police to stop them.

Well this worked for a time till Uncle Rob got smart and had his A-rabs come down there at midnight when the police and the Irishmen weren't there.

They had Mr. Bailey go up to talk to the owner of the coal yards early in the morning. Like I said from far away you couldn't tell if he was white or colored.

Well Cousin Bailey got in to see the owner who agreed to sell the coal (you no just a little bit higher then he sold it to the Irishmen). The agreement also was a contract that would be renewed each year starting in Aug till February.

Well like I said Mr. Bailey was a smart man who could make a good deal with any one and speak their language at the same time.

Man, I could just see him walking up to that office dressed up in a new suit and shined shoes and a hat that showed that he was a classy man.

I can imagine that it wasn't going to be easy to get the colored people to buy their coal. First most of them poor people were under the thumb with that time payment on the coal. Second most of them also trusted the Irishmen that delivered the coal.

What they needed was a gifted salesman. He had to go door to door and sale the idea of a colored coal company that would deliver the coal in any kind of weather.

He had to show the people that the colored coal company had the best price for them and that time payment was a way of keeping the colored people down.

One such man was a cousin of ours, Samuel Daniels on the Chase side of the family.

Well Mr. Daniels was a smoothed talker and when he had just one person in the neighborhood selling he gave them a discount on a month's worth of coal.

Now here is how they were beating the Irishmen, they would sale it by the week. You could buy a week's load and owe no one or you could buy a month's load and paid up front if you had that kind of money.

To help the people that were under the Irishmen's time payment they loaned the people the balance on their loan. The people would have to sign a contract that was up to the amount they owed the Irish and plus pay a quarter over what they owned the Irishmen.

Well this wasn't setting well with the Irish deliverymen who lost costumers.

Also Grandma wasn't too happy with the deal as well; in fact she was fit to be tied over the amount that Cliff used out of the Bar's profit.

Now if Big Cliff had used the family money it wouldn't have been too bad, but winter was coming and the Bar business would be down because of the bad weather.

She was wise enough to know that the only thing that they had to carry them over the winter was the rent coming from the boarding houses.

The lunch room business would be only the Afro- American newspaper lunch crowd and the few single people who worked late. The grocery store and her mothers that was across from hers would suffer as while. The road houses would be no business at all and the people down there would need to come back to the city for work in the winter.

So as not to lose them she had to come up with something real quick.

The first thing she did was put them folks up in the boarding houses; they would live free during the winter. Next she had the women working for Cliff's mother, doing laundry. The men would be sent to jobs with the rail road cooking or as trash men with Legs. The cooks would be used in the kitchen with the other cooks on the late shift. Now she still had all those different personalities to put up with.

It was a long time before Sarah started seeing once more Mr. Bernstein. They were still on talking terms and he wanted her to see the new Negro play that was opening at the playhouse.

Oh, can I go? She thought to herself, it was getting colder and in her new house she had the same heat as the white people gas heat.

Most of the family would go to her house just to get the smell of coal off of them. Cliff had the Gas Company come into the Bar and hook the entire house with gas and electric lights with A-base fuse boxes in the basement which cost him a lot. He told Rob Tolson to watch everything that the white gasman and electrician did.

Now Robert Tolson was one smart guy he not only, watched them but he offered to help them as while. When the gas line need to be run in a small space and the fat gasman could get his big behind in behind the wall, Rob went in and had the man hand him the pipes. The Gasman offered him a job helping him to install gas lines and meters in the white areas of Baltimore.

This left Cliff short a good man so he had to find someone to handle the beer and wine coming into the Bar in the early mornings.

Who would be better then the family next door, the McCrite's, which lived at 442 Orchard Street, George and Mary and their daughter Lucy who could work the morning shift at 7 am. The Weeks had a big son also that could help George in the basement named John.

Grandma would try to cover all sides if she could; she would just walk up to her neighbors and ask them if they needed a job or if they were looking for a new job. It was as simple as that, and with the weather getting colder it was nice to work so close to were you lived.

What amazed me more was the fact just two to three years after the war, there were so many German families still living on the even side of Druidhill Ave. You had the Friedman next to a family that were from Grandma's home the Jones next to them, would be the Levin family. The Hyman's next to them the Smallwood's who were black next to them on that block of two stories houses, where the rooms were no more then 9x9. Three small bedrooms with the small living room and kitchen all running to the larger back yards.

You would have Blacks and Jews living in harmony, so I know Grandma kept a descent place. That served white as well as black people food and drinks. This was Baltimore's 17th ward.

America is a nation at war with it's self, and we are a people that are at war with ourselves. Now the same illness that was in slavery is still imbedded within each of us. The short, the tall, the thin, the fat, and the dark and the light! The straight hair and the curly hair, we all are at war with one another.

Is it strange, was there not a war in Heaven, good vs. evil!

Well that's how life is in 1920 and today, it's the family that keeps us going and Grandma knew it, she saw it first hand in Virginia. In her own house, she saw what happens when an older man takes advantage of a younger woman. She had to live to knew how to handle the war in others. She saw it in Cliff, she knew of his daughter for he was only eighteen when it happened.

She knew that her mother was seeing someone and hiding it from the family. Nothing is done under the sun that hasn't already happened.

Negroes were also opening their own businesses in the Negro community; one was our cousin Mr. Daniels. He had an ice cream company named the Arundel Ice Cream Company after his home town.

My grandmother and our cousin Lorraine were tight as a tick on a hound dogs back. Them ole gal's would be on telephone, just like them gals do now, talking for hours everyday up to when my grandmother died. I can see them now just a talking up there in heaven.

So with Lorraine living and working in the lunchroom, she kept her eye on Cliff and my granddaddies cousin, that Chase boy. Now there was a good catch, one of them ole boys had a lunchroom and the other was the related to the son of a funeral home director. The home was just around the corner from the bar on Wilson street.

Man this was the Jazz age and Negroes were on the way up town!

It's simple to me that in the daytime Cliff served the colored people and after hours he served the white people.

Now the pool hall would draw the very high end of gamblers, those that felt that they had the edge on the other players by their skill and mastery of that game.

We all knew and saw the many movies of the pool hustlers of the depression era but the skill and money of the pool players of the twenties was very profound. If any one made a name for himself shooting pool it was ole Uncle Wabbet.

The young white crowd would come in, and in most cases they wanted what we call soul food or down home style cooking. Down home cooking was greasy and fried compared to up town meals which where baked and broiled.

Granddaddy had a crab cake recipe that couldn't be beat. He would take crab meat and mix the claws with lump meat and then he would add salt and pepper plus some Bay Island, just enough to make your mouth water not enough to burn. Then he would add to the mix, yellow mustard plus dry mustard, eggs and then roll the balls in flour or cracker crumbs that depended on who he was serving them too. Then he would have his lard nice and hot, and then he would put the cakes in the hot lard till golden brown.

71

With the weather changing this helped Grandma in her plan to keep the road house workers. To keep enough money to run this she had to make sure that the white crowd that came in, after hours were happy with what they served so she used the best cooks on the 11 pm shift. The road house menus were also used and the Chef Chief ran the after-hour night time shift.

But still she had more problems with who was going to work that after hour shift!

Now not far from my grandfather's place was his Great Uncles place the Chase Funeral Home now run by Mr. Chase's Great Grandson, on Wilson Street. He would be my grandfather's first cousin.

Now this to me was pretty amazing that the great Grandson of an Irish indentured servant and a free man of color could be able to do all of this in almost the worst conditions that this Nation has known, as far as race relations were concerned.

Now my Grandfather was not finished with things to do, he must have had the backing and I know that he had to be pushed along, not only by someone but also his family. Because you and I know that the food and the beer were under white control now.

I know that working on the railroad gave him the knowledge of the wholesalers of food and the kitchen equipment that he needed but the beer and wine came from the Italians of Southeast Baltimore that were moving up with the colored community.

The money that the Italians had made it easy for them to buy the houses of the rich white folks who were more than happy to sell them, than to live in the same community with poor colored people.

The Italians of Southeast Baltimore would buy these houses cheap and sell them high to the colored people, at the same time colored people were finding good paying jobs in the city that once denied them good jobs.

Colored people where doing things other than cleaning rich people homes and many were educated passed the six grades.

Due in part to these Bible schools whom now where training men and women to do other things besides cleaning and cooking for their living.

The white community was unknowingly supporting these Bible schools, thinking that they were only teaching bible studies.

It was also the policy makers that were pushing the colored community as well for in every Baptist Church on the daily reading board was the winning number for the week!

There were a lot of people that went to Church just to get the weekly number. Now you might think that, that was so wrong but if you take the time and think on it you would see that those people that came would have never joined the church or heard the promise that the Lord said "come as you are." Nor would they know that to be saved, all you had to do was call on the name of the Lord and believe that he, Jesus is lord and that he died, and was raised from the grave.

Not only that but many of these large Churches were developing a social Class that fed good men into not only the Masons but other organizations that were not open to Negroes.

Negroes then where making all kinds of changes to the area that up till then was never heard of.

Negro replaced the term colored people and there were movie houses opening up by the Jews for Negroes to keep them out of the movie houses down town on Howard Street.

Education was getting off the ground as well with the opening of Fredrick Douglass High School located at Saratoga near Charles Street that was up town. Then a one year teaching course was setup in that old building and the name of the school that gave that course was Coppin Teachers College.

Now in 1894 the great Fredrick Douglass gave the first Commencement address. One year after Big Cliff was born! We were moving up from slavery to a modern people. In just fifty-five years.

Frederick Douglass said at that Commencement address "The colored people of this country have, I think, made a great mistake, of late, in saying so much of race and color as a basis of their claims to justice, and as the chief motive of their efforts and action. I have always attached more importance to manhood than to mere identity with any variety of the human family..." "We should never forget that the ablest and most eloquent voices ever raised in behalf of the black man's cause were the voices of white men. Not for race, not for color, but for men and for manhood they labored, fought, and died. Away, then, with the nonsense that a man must be black to be true to the rights of black men."

Fredrick Douglass High School then moved up town on the west side to a building on the corner of Dolphin Street and Pennsylvania Avenue in 1900. Now Negroes were able to go to school close to their homes that were taking over that area.

Also Centenary Biblical Institute (now Morgan Collage) was also one of the first Negro Bible Schools that was putting out a new kind of Negro, free from the chains of slavery and the Jim Crow laws.

Pennsylvania Ave was also the site in 1799, which the first group of Black slaves from Haiti settled near the unit block of Pennsylvania Avenue at Franklin Street to help build the St. Mary's Seminary. That was the first school that Brother Larry and I were put out of by Black nuns!

Well back to the life and times of Big Cliff!

Grandma had Miss Bessie working the after-hours crowd. It was because she wasn't related to us and she was older than the rest of them.

Chapter 10

Now at this time my Uncle Robert (Wabbet) was doing great down on the south side of town. He was planning to move up town near his younger brother Alonzo where he would have some new connections and new customers leaving the south side routes to Mr. Queen.

With more colored people moving up on the west side and southeast side of town near better neighborhoods the need for good food was much more needed by the hard working folks that were seen in and out of the spoon's. But the spoon was not the place were you would take ones family! With the twenties roaring in my Grandfather started selling glasses of beer that came from the brewers down near Little Italy.

Now selling beer and wine at the spoon in 1919 got pretty good. It called for my Granddaddy to hire a man that was big enough to throw someone out of the place if he got out of control.

There was one man that he knew from the Railroad his name was Albert Murdock he was the house bouncer and night bar tender.

Grandma's cousin Lawrence Tolson had a good idea and he wrote Grandma about it, he was going to ship all that he had grown that summer to Baltimore on one of them new freezer cars. The fresh fruit would be shipped on another car. The problem would be trucks to get to the train station and drivers and the rail cars that they could put their produce. He thought that his idea had merit but Grandma wrote back telling him that with all the connections the family had they could not get around the fact that white America would not let black people ship any thing between the states by rail.

Lawrence was determined, not to take no for an answer so he went to Baltimore to talk to Cliff. Once he and his cousin Nat came, they told Cliff what they thought was a good idea.

"Look Cliff, we aren't making anything on all that food we grow down there. The white people pay us what they want on our produce. And we don't have machinery to work the land like we should. If we had the new tractors and farm equipment we could enlarge our farms. Most of the farmers down there are still share choppers owing the white landowners more than they can produce".

"I see what you boys mean it's a problem of transportation to get them to a payable market. Tell you what I think." said Cliff. "I got a buddy who owns a barge and I will tell him, if he can get that barge down the Potomac River".

"Yea that will work I can drive my wagons to Brent's Landing and unload them on to the barge." said Lawrence.

"I use to know an ole boy down there who I taught to cook. His name is, Amos, yea, Amos Burnett." said Cliff.

"Oh Mr. Amos, your brother in- law, works for Leonard R Tolson!"

"Yea, he married your wife's Aunt".

"Yes that's right Bessie Tolson, yea that's my wife's Aunt." said Cliff.

"Yea, her father's daughter." said Nat, "our Aunt".

"You boys get that food to Brent's landing and I will do the rest and the profit from the food I send back Weston Union.

Now this took all the pull or influence that Cliff had in ole man Williams, a white man that he knew when he was sailing up and down the Chesapeake Bay.

Once the produce got to Baltimore, Cliff had to get the Italians in Little Italy to haul it to the stores up on Druid Hill Ave. With the fields bear now in Heathsville, the cousins were hoping that times would be easier for them.

"It's a hard reality when one race wouldn't let another race survive with simple commerce." said Larry Tolson.

Cliff said, "To change the subject he would never forget who brought them up here, Gertrude (Grandma) and her small family, it was on Franklin Street, the 700 block. He said that his mother and half sisters and step-father and half brothers lived down the Street from them at 505 Franklin. He couldn't help but see the young beauty and knowing that she was a country gal made it even better to him. They were living with James Bailey and Aunt Lezzy and their little niece Dorothy Taylor. He said they were all looking for a job the best people that he could have hired then".

"Lawrence, if you are any thing like them I know that this is going to turn out fine." he said

"Yea every year about this time our people suffer the hardest, the chops are in and all we got is Mules to pull the wagons and the children walking behind them picking the produce. You know most of them younglings would rather work picking Tobacco than food. Them white farmers pay them more then we ever could. Man if we had tractors we could do much better and not burn up our land."

Sarah thought to herself, do I have second sight, maybe to some degree. She remembered her late husband use to talk about his older sister and how she took over running the farm after their mother remarried. Margaret A Laws married into the Toliferro family when she was thirty seven years old and had two more children and left the up keep of Tom Tolson's farm to Sophronia Tolson. Sophronia was twenty five years old then.

Just when she was getting into her own mind there was a knock at her door. She would often spend the quiet evening setting in her large living room thinking. Who might that be she thought to herself?

Just then Mary came in and told her, "Mama there's a white man to see you!"

"Wait! Wait!" Sarah cried out. She slipped on a kimono, wrapped her hair hastily, shoved her feet into some slippers, and walked to the parlor door.

There at the door was a large and heavy set man of about fifty, with grizzled and graying hair and skin.

"Pardon me, my name is Captain Galion Williams, I'm a friend of Cliff Seeney. He gave me this address and told me that you would be interested in what we are doing!"

78

A very surprised look was on her face, "What are you talking about?" She thought, now I guess that proves I don't have second sight.

"Well, Madam, me and Cliff got together with some ole boys from your home and we got a barge load of produce and if the weather gets cold tonight that there stuff will just be all wasted. I need a large place big enough to store it. You see Cliff had some trucks to pick some of it up but there still plenty of it still on my barge."

"Well, what can I do?" she said

"Well, he said that you had a place were we could put the bags of produce in till he gets his brother to get his people to haul the food around town and sell it."

"Ok, I do, it's;" she thought to her self that big building that belongs to Mrs. McCormack. She was showing off, showing us what her husband has driving us all around town in her limo. How did he know she questioned herself, or maybe he was just hoping I had a place?

"Ok, you unload the barge to all the trucks and wagons that you have and if you need any more wagons rent them. Here let me go get some money so that you can rent them."

Taking all the money that she had saved in the house she gave it to this unknown white man and told him to meet her down on Paca Street as soon as he had unloaded his barge.

"Oh, excuse me again Madam, here's a receipt for your money."

"Oh, thank you very much I wasn't thinking."

"My name is Christophe Galion Williams and Miss it's really a pleasure meeting you".

"Oh, thank you very much for helping us out like this." she said. "That will keep us with a lot of produce in the winter. Let me call Mrs. McCormack now!

After she got the keys from Mrs. McCormack's chauffeur, she was off and running using the chauffeur to drive her down to the Warehouse.

My God think of it me, driving in a Limousine, driven by a young good looking black driver I do hope the neighbors see me she thought.

Sarah also received news that her half sister was living on Wilson Street with her In-laws the Nickens family, George C and his wife and family plus his Brother- in law Morris T Paul.

We were never close because my mother was black and her mother was a Mulatto. That's ok because we do have the same daddy and his blood is in me not my mothers she thought.

Once she arrived at the warehouse the trucks and wagons were all lined up in the alley. Ready to unload the fruit and vegetables before the frost hit them. She could feel the cold and she knew that Cliff was indeed lucky this night and she knew that she would have lost her life saving on this hair brain idea.

Later Cliff took some of the men up stairs to an office and told them that he didn't know how long they would have this warehouse.

"Listen, you guys Miss Sarah got us this here place; now I don't know how long we can operate out of here. We will just keep them A-Rabs of Robert supplied with fresh produce all winter with this and the shipments down at Curtis bay." Cliff said. "The man that is going to run this warehouse boys will be John Bailey and Monroe Walker, we will help him. They might not be known to all of you but Robert grew up with them and they are my cousins. They all are from the 700 block of Franklin Street. Now we got to keep this place a secret till we get someone down to city hall an get us a license to run this place till then try not to let the word get out that some colored men are running a produce market in down town Baltimore."

Cliff went up town to talk to his mother-in-law about how long they would be able to use that huge warehouse. Not only was it being used to bring in the Cubans produce but he was using it to stock beer barrels and wine barrels. The mob wanted him to sell whiskey as well, but he kept putting them off. He would tell them that his National Guard duties kept him from using any thing that was illegal. Also the National Guard duties were now taking up a lot of his time, but he was able to keep up with his many business enterprises because of Grandma.

Grandma would run the Bar in the morning till noon, till he came in and ran the night crew. She would then go downtown to check on the warehouse and see that the books were straight. Then she would head back up town on the trolley car to check on little Cliff. Once she was at her mother's house she asked about the warehouse.

"Mama, Cliff asked me to ask you how long can they use the warehouse?"

"Well sweetie", her mother started calling all her children that. "Well, I got the use of it till Cliff pays me back the money I fronted him on it. And then we can buy it out right through my Lawyer, Herman. He will have to buy it for us." she said.

"Ok mama that will be great. I will let Cliff know and I'm sure he will get on that money quick." Grandma said.

"Herman" Grandma thought to herself MMMMMMM!

As the winter started in 1920 it came after a mild fall but it started very cold and the vegetables were all sold out thanks to the quick thinking of Great Grandmother Sarah, and Granddaddy Cliff.

Chapter 11

There was a system, which came down from the big cities to the north, older than time. The lottery, numbers they called it in those days, policy slips.

Now the colored men, as they were called in them days, held most of these small time policy slips (numbers). One of the same colored men would become a hero to many who lived in the eastern counties of Baltimore; they called him Little Willie Adams in the thirties to his early forties. But I'm getting a little ahead of the story.

We had baseball teams ran by policy slips that paid the players and kept the selling of tickets cheap and we were able to build a ball park in the West Port area of South Baltimore near pig town.

Now men like Mr. Adams wasn't little but the meaning was that it was little because their policy slips paid very little money compared to the Italian mob slips that paid off more.

The results was the Italian mob winning numbers where posted in the Sunday Sun Newspaper in the Race section under the 9th race at Pimlico Racetrack. The results were always the winning three horse numbers in that race.

That not only sold newspapers but a lot of people, poor people, started to go out to the track every day to play the races and transportation there was improved.

It got so good that the white people and colored people where both playing the Races and the numbers as the Italians called it. Now they, the Italian mob had a day-to-day number not just that Sunday number.

And yes that did stop a lot of people from going to Church, where the preachers were asking for 10% of their incomes. You might think that the bible says that we should give 10% but a lot of people didn't have that kind of Faith or money.

Now most of the banks, the illegal banks (the booking houses), that paid off on the winning numbers were ran by the Italians, who had colored people running or booking the numbers for them. Now I can't say for sure whether or not my Grandfather ran or was the bank but one thing is for sure he was Mr. Al Capone's Godson.

So you would have to take it from there yourself with the number of people coming into his lunch room and Pool hall and the grocery stores and all the places that they had it would be more than likely that he was the bank and my Great Uncle's were the runners on the day to day numbers.

Now one of the fastest pay off numbers in Black Baltimore was the Lodge number of the Masonic Lodge # 945 or was it 459 any ways box it and see does it pay. I had a buddy that hit it in 1975 for 600 dollars in a box at 6to 1, odds $36,000 dollars. Yea brought himself some good property and a night club up on Charles Street.

And them meaning, any one that had many people coming to one location or many locations that would be the best place to collect the nickels and dimes that people played on numbers. Man you would have old Miss Mabel come in and say put this her penny on 621and box it.

Now most of the big money that was coming into the lunchroom would be coming from the sale of beer and wine and the numbers. That meant that Cliff could move out to his dream of opening up a place near Annapolis where the well to do colored people could (now, here's a modern term just eighty-seven years ago) drive down and spend a day or two at his new lodge by the bay that he would later call Green Pastures after the famous Colored movie. He knew just where in Anne Arundel County he was going to put his dream, it was near Brooklyn Park.

That area would be down near the water that they now call Curtis Bay.

I guess it was near enough to Baltimore and far enough that it would take a few hours drive, now that they where building a major highway to Annapolis called the Annapolis Road.

This road ran though a small Negro community called West Port then it went south following a road that went to Hanover Street then back into Baltimore city.

Mr. Albert had his Cubans build a pier down near where the lodge would be located which was ideal for what he was doing as far as the Cuban gals where concerned.

Brown sugar was the thing back in them there days. There was nothing sweeter to a longshoreman, than a taste of Brown sugar. Those hard working men would sometimes give a weeks wage to taste a little brown sugar. Which became a poplar song in the sixties, by many artists but it was a sung by these longshoreman years ago.

There were now many Cuban females living on the west side of town. The Cuban sailors that were on the many Cuban ships that were bringing the bananas up to Baltimore started to jump ship on a regular basis. That started the large Cuban community that was located up town near Fulton Ave and Reisterstown Road. One of the biggest events in Baltimore out at Druid Hill Park use to be the Afro-Cuban festival that as of late the name was changed to Afram. I thought I would bring that up now that I'm talking about the Cubans. My granddaddy didn't have much to do with them but his younger half brother did. It wasn't long before his younger brother stopped messing with them because of the dangerous men that they drew to them. Just like flies, and you know what! Now the many mixed race Cubans were well known by many in the old days, many lived next door to us in the fifties. As time changed so did people, the Cubans became the poor whites whom were dark skinned living mostly in Northeast Baltimore.

Now my Grandfather was not finished with things to do, he must have had the backing of someone that would benefit from the expansion of his many enterprises. I know that he had to be pushed along not only by someone in his family but I feel that he got interested in them road houses as a way to sell booze.

My granddaddy knew a lot of people and some of them were very important people in the white community who needed outlets for their own simple pleasures, not every thing is rosy and nice! He was privy to the knowledge of the inner workings of the railroad concerning food service. That gave him the knowledge to the wholesalers of food and the kitchen equipment that he needed but the beer and wine came from the Italians of Southeast Baltimore that were moving up with the colored community in the early years of the roaring twenties. At the same time that the social order was changing so was the Church.

In 1906 on the west cost of this country a great Church movement was started and it was headed east. Many of these new preachers were riding the railroad from the west coast to the great cities on the east coast. My Granddaddy would meet many of them after the long ride on the train. That would give them a chance to preach to the colored workers on that train. Now they were preaching almost the same thing that the Baptist Church was, the only difference was they were now saying that there was proof that you were saved! And to many the weekly visit by the Baptist preacher would not be needed, but now it would be a daily visit to the tents that these here Preachers were putting up.

My father would tell me how there was a preacher that started a divine movement that was sweeping the new colored community, and one person that they were pointing to was the man that was leading them down that wide road,well you know who it was, Big Cliff. Since my granddaddy owned them road houses that had female dancers and sold beer these here preachers just had too pick on him since they couldn't pick on anyone else. So my granddaddy made peace with them by cutting out Sunday hooch dancing and the sale of beer and wine on Sunday. Since most of the black deacons would find themselves at his road houses after Church. The one man that daddy would talk about was a man that called himself Father Divine, this man had long hair, straight black and wore white robes and called his followers Joy and Peace and Faithful and so now most all of his members were women. Now if I could see something wrong there and I was just a young boy, I know that others did as while.

Well that didn't stop granddaddy from making a dollar off of that, he would have specials just for them Sunday chicken dinners. Fried chicken that you could smell ten to twenty miles away!

And after them long gospel meetings Father Divine had and now a new guy from New York named Daddy Grace had the people jumping around and falling out like they were under his spell. Much like the Voodoo priest in New Orleans! This here thing was nothing new to my granddaddy because the Haitians on Orchard Street had been doing that since they came here back in the early part of the last century.

What was thought by many of the newly arrived people from North and South Carolina as the Holy Spirit falling on them was just a trance that these here new preachers were putting on them. So my granddaddy didn't get involved with that and he made sure most of the family kept their distance from these tent meetings. Well, just like everything else you always had that one who saw a dollar in it. Well, what they did was to find open lots around the Pen North area and they brought them from the owners at a very low cost and they rented them there lots to these here preachers for their meetings. Now this was getting to be very profitable to one of my Uncles.

He would have them buy his clean white gowns and things as while and the notice that the lunch room was open after the meetings for Sunday suppers. And the preacher's meal was free.

Those people were packing the lunch room every Sunday and they were now running out of food. So my granddaddy thought that he needed a partner in the lunch room business.

Now they had crabs that could full the biggest pot up and they had all kinds of fish down there in Curtis Bay but one thing they had was shad fish and Big Cliff was the king when it came to cooking shad. They said that he could make the bones melt on any fish.

With a little salt and a little pepper and the right shorting and the right kind of flour and lets not forget some hot source what you say sure you right.

I tell you them boys down in New Orleans would come up here just to get a little smell of it and if you had a little smile with you whom James Martin always had then the party was on.

Now the band be playing rag and the gals they be just wiggling and you know that Aunt Hattie with them big brown legs would just be carrying on. The whole family would be there Grandmother and her mama, my old aunts long passed my Uncles with their different styles would be there just a smiling my Aunt Bee would be just a cooking any thing that was right was right in her pots, for Uncle Wabbet found himself the right gal in Ant Bee.

My great Uncle Isiah would have his people with him and maybe some of them ole Chase's would happen by down on the Shady side.

The Laws and Nickens, the Taylors and Tolson's would be there, the Brooks and the Monroe's would be in the crowd. Maybe some of them Delaware Seeney's would show up with them Moor's, the Daniel's and the place would be rocking to the sound of Jazz.

Ole Louie from New Orleans would bring his horn to play and those new boys would be playing the keyboard just like it was church!

Down on the shady side!

My grandfather's place that was now down in Glen Burnie was now the home to the entertainers headed to all parts north and south that they started calling the chittlins circuit.

Now Cliff learned that when you help people, good thing come back on you, and one hand always washes the other. He learned that by watching his father's brother Uncle Isiah. His Uncle was his teacher and like I said before if the Lord is for you who can be against you. Someone probably taught him, so the cycle keeps going.

I hope and pray that someone will come along in our family and renew the spirit of Big Cliff for we need it now more then ever.

Big Evelyn Monroe

Now my Granddaddy also had a sister that was near his own age that we all called Big Evelyn Monroe, who was born in Baltimore. After her other brothers were pretty well established in Baltimore she would also work for the family in one of the many spoons that Big Cliff had popping up all over the south and west side of Baltimore.

Now she was the one that my Grandmother Gertrude, when she came up from Virginia, looked up too and she was a great help in getting my Grandmother accustomed to life in the big city.

It was always a great joy to see my Grandmother Gertrude (as we called her Grandma Gurdie) it was Evelyn (now a Brooks) who penned that name on my Grandmother, she was a very proper lady who referred to my Grandmother as Gurdie.

Grandma would get herself prepared to go up on Gwynfalls Parkway and see Big Evelyn. My Grandmother would put on this real expense perfume that had a rose scent to it. And she would have the best dress that she got from the Hecht Company which in them days, even when I was young, was the rich white folk's store.

She my Grandmother would have on the walking out dress of a rich and successful colored woman. She would catch the uptown trolley car to Gwynfalls Parkway; it was a real joy when my grandma would take my brother Larry and I up on the rail car to see her. This rich colored woman would get such a joy seeing us. The only thing was we hated to dress up and we couldn't wait to take our school clothes off.

You see, once Evelyn Monroe got old enough, her brother Cliff got her a job working in one of the best families (White that is) in Baltimore. He met Mr. Carroll on one of his trips and Mr. Carroll asked him for reference on a top-notch housekeeper.

Not only was she a top-notch housekeeper but also she went to College later in life and got a good education.

There's not much more that I know on her but the Brooks were what we call the new Black bourgeoisie.

She married a man name Brooks and now this stately lady was a key or leading member of the Brooks family. She had two children one boy who would later become the commander of Civil Defense for Baltimore City and a one star General as well. Her daughter was a well know worker at the Social Security Offices from downtown Baltimore to their new offices in Woodlawn. Her grandson is one of the nation's top photographers.

Cliff knew now that he had to get his thoughts together. He saw how his younger brothers where doing well and moving away and setting up on there own. Brother Robert was now the Sheriff of the pony boys in south Baltimore.

Ole Uncle Wabbet was the leader of the A-rabs and he did it all on his own but he still keep close to his oldest brother. His younger brother was the great up town ladies man. Cliff's best friend uncle Jimi was known up and down the Southside of town. When people disappeared some would say that they must have crossed ole Jimi or stepped on his shoes, them black and whites that he wore all the time or those Stacey Adams wing tips.

Case in point; once my Granddaddy started to get big, as far as money goes, everybody that didn't have any wanted him to give them some of his. Now let me tell you how we Negroes started to think that way.

The only way that most Negro's learned to read and write was the bible. So many people from the south could remember the whole word or phrase and associated it with writing. That is the way most Negroes back then only spoke with words from the bible they could memorize, whole phrases and then they learned to put them together for the common every day speech.

Now the Bible said that it was easier for a camel to go through an eye of a needle than a rich man to get into Heaven. So they all thought that if you gave your money away you were sure to go to Heaven.

Now that's just my thoughts and not my granddaddy for what he did for people was from his love of life.

He was happy when he could help someone, so many people that couldn't buy a hot cake on Monday could eat a hot cake on Monday and when they came back on Tuesday they brought something to Cliff, to pay for all them Monday's, they called them cakes the "Monday cakes".

They would come in the spoon and order a "Monday cake" and everyone that worked in the spoon knew what that meant. Give me a Monday Cake!

Now the preachers were always getting and very few were giving so most folks back in them days stayed away from Church. Once they left their homes in the South and like the saying goes went buck wild.

Well it was hard for a Preacher to get them back in the Church once they were in Egypt (the world or in this case Baltimore). So the new style of Preachers which called themselves Holiness had to always do something to the people or for them to keep them in the church. Now my granddaddy also saw how they were competing with one another for members. He knew that if he wanted to stay up on things that he would have to ally himself with one of them there new preachers.

Now the old AME Church that was around on Orchard Street was a good place to start and since his family was getting larger it was the right thing to do so he had my grandmother going there. He wasn't able to go himself because he had to be out on the road to keep them road houses running. Now once my grandmother started going to that famous church that had the Underground Railroad in its basement the members were more than welcome around at the lunchroom or her mother's place that was a lot quieter than the bar.

Many of the people that were up here in Baltimore were from the same farming towns in the south. They would come up here thinking that they were free from the chains that had them bound in the south. They didn't know that they were going to exchange those chains for new ones. Yes, it would be true that the treatment by the white population would be different due to their numbers, but they brought the same class separation here. What they brought is called Colorism. Now grandaddy knew of this in his travels in the US Navy. He knew that he could benefit from it and use it as a tool to move and motivate people.

He would have a light skinned person working doing manual labor and a dark skinned person doing what they called book work. This gave him a chance to include any one with real talent in his endeavors. That also set him up to fall because of his indifference with certain people. Now many of the people newly come to Baltimore were thinking that they were free from that down home religion. They were now the free from the fear that something bad was going to happen to them if they didn't act right. So Big Cliff was kind of like their Priest, when things got bad and they needed some hot cakes on Monday to get them through till that next Monday they would go see Big Cliff. So long as Big Cliff did well the people that knew him would do good as well when times got hard. So when the rich white and Jewish landlords would go up on their rent and the man or woman that they work for didn't pay them enough to pay that rent Big Cliff had a place that they could rent for what they made.

Now I always wondered why they called him big Cliff was it his size or was it something else like he was the senior member of his family and my daddy was the junior.

I met a woman that knew she told me because he had Big Money and my daddy had little money and I have less than both because my daddy couldn't add to his daddy's money when he was gone.

Well not only that, my Granddaddy was big because of what he did for others you often heard "that was big of him"!

So the people around him profit from his life and his giving spirit.

Were the people trusting in the Lord, yes they were but they were trusting in a new and different way.

This way was new from what they were use to in the South and when they were on the farm and when they went to church to hear that "sweet by and by preaching".

Just like Ole Moses could not cross into the promise land with the ole ways and them ole ways could not cross after into it as well. God had to rise up a new leader to carry his people over the river Jordan. Jesus was sent that we could move from the ole laws to the new grace.

Now the streets were paved with Gold and the gold was his people, you just had to know how to get the gold out of them.

Now my uncle James was no different than Caleb who told the Lord "give me this mountain" and Caleb went and took that Mountain.

My Uncle James was not the kind of a man that didn't believe that the Lord went before him and that nothing was impossible for him to do. Nor was my granddaddy for both were men after the Lords own heart.

They didn't let the times or the problems of those times stop them for they saw the glory of the Lord over and over in their lives. Every day the Lord made away where there was no way. And opened doors that were closed and closed doors that where open.

So everyday was better to them than the day before because they knew that the Lord of JOSHUA went before them and the battle was his not theirs.

The Bible says that Jesus asked a man once 'how do you see men' and that man said 'I see men as trees in a forest.' After Jesus worked on that man's vision he asked that man again. How do you see men, that man said, I see men as your creation I see man with your glory around them, I see man as streets paved in Gold.

That's how my granddaddy saw his people as streets paved in Gold and all you had to do was feed his people and do right by them, help that one till he can help himself.

There's no such thing as God helps the one that has his own, his own what for all of this belongs to him so what is it that belongs to you, nothing. So how can he help someone with nothing?

He is the one that helps you out of that bed in the morning; he is the one that carries you to the bathroom to relive yourself of the world that's in you and killing you.

It's him that made us and not we ourselves; we are his tools that work for his benefit not for our own benefit. Lord you got me preaching, it should say God helps the child that has him in their heart!

Now Big Cliff was not always Big Cliff till God started working in his life, he was making all things happen in this man's life. Like the people said, he must be living right.

I can't attest to that but one thing is for sure and that is if the Lord be for you who can be against you. Now when I was growing up my daddy always had a job for every one in the neighborhood, and when you where broke you could always depend on him giving you a good paying job till you where out of the hole that in most cases you dug for yourself.

Now that meant that my daddy had to be out there doing the right thing by the people that he worked for. Now if it wasn't for his fast and good work we wouldn't have a job and earn some fast easy money that was legal and since if the Lord is for you who can be against you! The same things happen to me, now once I got grown and on my own I had myself a job that I had to hire others to help me. So at one time I had three or four men helping me sell papers, the Sunday Sun and the place where we sold these papers was, yea you guessed it was on Druid Hill Ave. And I had one also on Franklin Street and also around Pennsylvania Ave and as far as Mt Royal Terrance, close to 2000 Sunday papers each week.

Life goes in a circle and God is ever before us making a way for us and when it was time for me to leave that kind of thing he opened a door that I could go through.

Life is funny that way and if it's in the blood it will come out. Now one thing was for sure most times things will have to be learned and though the main problem that we have now days, and I just as guilty as the next man, is we are not teaching our young the lessons that we were taught. Is it because we want more than our parents had, is it that we are just too darn lazy. Well, I say we are just too busy and lazy now days. We spend most of our time trying to impress others and most times the one we should be impressing are our own family members. Now it is with out a doubt that Big Cliff was a hard worker not in laboring to improve his family but tireless in his endeavors to build up on the things that he had and he knew that what ever he did would improve every one in his family. I see him reaching out to cousins who were second and third cousins, forth and some times fifth cousins. If he had something, they all had something! With the help of is Grandfather's Beverly Laws and Samuel Chase he was able to reach beyond his own abilities. Now I once saw how it was done if someone has something that they want to do and if you know that you can improve on it give that person a helping hand just don't leave them hanging on to the side of the boat. Now in writing a book it takes the help of someone willing to set and read every page with the eye of an editor. Willing to give time and help someone who in my case needed a steady hand in the deep waters of life. Helping me along with the small details spelling and grammar! Just as it was for big Cliff it is for all people the Bible says that he has given some one talent and another two. Well once that one took his talent and used it he was given more and the one that didn't use his lost the one he had. Now I'm in no way saying that we should just give a person anything but we should help to move that person along with encouragement and praise for what they are doing. That was big Cliff's way; always moving someone along in their life.

To be continued!!! Look for Book Three this summer The Blood and the name Mesi Kliff Marbot (Cliff I Seeney). Please read the New Adventures of Marbot on line free Part one and two at the NWC and the INWC or just write in the books name!